Dedication

To Emer, who spots all my little mistakes

A Word from the Editor

It's not every day that the Portadown Tourist Board flies someone out to New York to discuss a publishing deal over a $4,000 brunch. In fact this generally only happens about once a year, and even then only when the Stormont Public Accounts Committee is suspended. Yet here I was, looking across the table at the curiously self-satisfied face of my host.

'So how would you feel about putting out a Portadown News book, Emerson?' asked Chairman G.W. Birdman, as the waiter skilfully poured two glasses of Chateau Catholique Nouveau Riche '98.

'Cheese board?' asked the waiter.

'No, Tourist Board,' replied Mr Birdman impatiently. 'I have my own printing company you know,' he continued quickly, 'They do all our leaflets and I get a stake.'

'Well done,' said the waiter.

'Tender on the inside,' explained Mr Birdman, waving him away. 'The thing is,' continued the Chairman, leaning conspiratorially over the table, 'we strongly believe that Portadown has enormous potential for tourism. It has international brand name recognition on a par with the great cities of the world. And publishing a book like *The Portadown News* could tap into that market.'

'Surely you don't believe that Portadown will ever be a major holiday destination?' I asked, after I had stopped choking.

'Well, of course not,' replied the Chairman not unkindly, 'but I do believe it has the potential for potential believability.'

'I'm sorry,' I said, 'I don't understand.'

'Then let me draw you a diagram,' said the Chairman, laying out a napkin and pulling out an Ulster Museum dinosaur pencil. 'Everything in Northern Ireland exists somewhere on a continuous circle of faith, like so. At the top of the circle is what we believe, then it progresses clockwise to what we'd like to believe, then what we say we believe, then what we know we should believe and finally what we think we believe, which is of course the same as what we actually believe, thus completing the circle.'

'Which means…?' I asked.

'Which means that if we'd like to believe in a tourist industry then we should say that we do believe in it and tell people we know that they should believe in it until we start thinking we really do believe in it at which point we actually will believe in it.'

'If only David Trimble had known about this,' I mused, 'things could all have worked out very differently.'

'Well if you believe that, then you should definitely say so,' replied the Chairman. 'But you must also believe in the potential of Portadown. It is a magical birthplace of new traditions. It is a melting-pot of Portuguese and non-Portuguese people. It is generally upwind of Lurgan. My boy – it is the hub of the North!'

'That would certainly explain all the spokesmen,' I said.

'Oh dear, oh dear,' said the Chairman, his voice tinged with disappointment. 'Shouldn't you be taking this a bit more seriously?'

Credits

With thanks to Graham Cordner for original programming, David Cordner for charitable hosting, Diarmuid Kennedy for graphic generosity, Henry McDonald for fearless reporting, John O'Farrell for publishing to be damned, Malachi O'Doherty for timely encouragement, Chris Lindsay for endless encouragement, Grania McFadden for getting me a job, Greg Harkin for giving me a job, Mum and Dad for office supplies, and everyone in Portadown who saw the funny side – especially Brian Courtney.

The Portadown News

9TH MARCH 2001   www.PortadownNews.com

Headcount 2001

IT'S THE PORTADOWN NEWS ELECTION SPECIAL!

The ballots have been printed, the speeches have been written, the alcopop bottles have been filled with smuggled petrol. Yes – election fever has gripped Portadown. Once again the good people of our beloved town ask that all-important question: "Are there still more Protestants than Catholics?"

To guide you through the difficult decisions that lie ahead, namely, "What **kind** of Protestant or Catholic are you?", we've asked the candidates to summarise their positions.

IDENTIFY YOURSELF!

It's important to bring the correct identification with you when you go to vote. To accommodate Portadown's social diversity, a wide range of documentation is now acceptable:

Electoral Ward A	Electoral Ward B
British Passport	Irish Passport
TV licence	Court summons
Mortgage statement	Rent arrears notice
Wage slip	UB40
Gun licence	Gun

HOW TO VOTE

Peaceful political participation can be confusing for many people in Portadown, and the proportional representation system only complicates matters. The Portadown News has compiled this handy cut-out-and-keep guide to voting in Northern Ireland:

1 As you approach the polling station, accept all leaflets offered to you. These people will remember your face.
2 Say hello to the policeman or 'community representative' guarding the door.
3 Point at any UN Observers present and shout, "Shouldn't you be in Zimbabwe?"
4 Show your identification to the nice old lady.
5 Receive your ballot, noting with alarm the unique serial number printed on the bottom.
6 Enter the booth, and savour the illusion of power.
7 Write '1' beside the candidate who has threatened you most recently.
8 Write '2' beside a moderate candidate, so you can kid yourself you're not **really** as bigoted as everyone else in this town.
9 Write '3' beside the Women's Coalition candidate, because they could use a bit more talent on 'Newsline'.
10 Think to yourself, "That'll change the fucking world, eh?"

Note: Sinn Fein voters should repeat this procedure until their bus leaves for the next constituency.

DAVID TREMBLE

Ulster Unionist Party

Portadown holds a special place in my heart. After all, I wouldn't be party leader if I hadn't caused all that trouble at Drumcree back in 1995. Now piss off.

MARVIN CURRIE

Democratic Unionist Party

The message I'll be taking to Westminster is: "Pope John Paul is The Antichrist." Once the English understand that, their whole attitude to Ulster will change.

AOIFE ROTTER

SDLP

I'll be continuing our policy of saying nice things on TV, while secretly plotting the downfall of civilisation. Tiocfaidh Ar La!

BRENDAN PUPPET

Sinn Fein

I'll ensure that the Catholic people of Portadown never again feel intimidated by their Protestant neighbours. Intimidating Catholics is our job.

JOHN HOGAN

Alliance

I'll be having some friends around for a meal, then watching the results on Newsnight. You're not invited.

TOM BELGIUM

Worker's Party

After the all-Ireland socialist revolution, there'll be peace and jobs for everyone. Also, Christmas will be the way it was when you were little, and it will only ever rain at night.

BARBARA MENARY

Women's Coalition

You don't need a dick to succeed in Ulster politics. You just need to **BE** a dick.

'Jesus votes DUP' – claim

by our religious affairs correspondent, Helen Brimstone

Jesus would vote DUP, claims Ivan Parsley, High Priest at Portadown's Bethany First Presbyterian Church. The controversial claim was made during Mr Parsley's Sunday sermon.

"The signs are clear, to the righteous," screamed Mr Parsley from his pulpit. "Jesus was unemployed, lived with his mum, hung around with his mates all day talking politics, and was always getting into trouble with the Romans. Clearly he was a DUP supporter."

However a spokesperson for the Electoral Commission has denied Mr Parsley's claims. "Mr Christ has been removed from the voting register," she told us, "as he has been dead for 1,972 years."

THE ISSUES

Health, education, transport: These are the issues we'd be voting on if we lived in a normal country. But as the candidates know we'll be voting along purely sectarian lines, they'll be careful not to raise these subjects during the campaign. To remind our readers of what will be happening behind the scenes while we continue our 400-year-old pointless argument, we've taken a closer look at the stories that really affect our lives.

WARDS MAY CLOSE

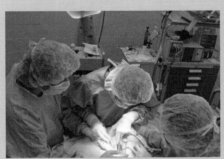

In-patient services at Craigavon Hospital are under threat again after the Health Trust spent £250,000 on a coffee machine for the trustees' boardroom. The hand-built gold-plated Italian machine is the first of its kind in Northern Ireland, delivering what some experts have described as:

"A blend to die for."

After a public meeting yesterday in Portadown Golf Club's Strictly Private Room, the Health Trust issued a statement defending its decision.

"We appreciate that people without private health insurance might be worried by this development," said the statement. "However we would remind the public that when you've to work late into the afternoon appointing your wives and boyfriends to health quangos, you need the best damn coffee money can buy."

SMALLER CLASS SIZES

Education Minister Martin McGuinness has promised to halve class sizes across Northern Ireland. Over the summer holidays, contractors will install wooden partitions in classrooms, bringing the average class size down from 600 sq.ft to 300 sq.ft.

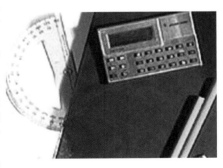

"As you know, I'm no fan of partition, but budgets have to be cut," explained Mr McGuinness yesterday. "Once people had jobs AND children, but now they tend to have either jobs OR children. Consequently it is unfair to make working people pay for schools."

The Education Minister's new programme has received the support of Dr Penny Guardian, Professor of Sociology at Queen's University. "Only stupid, lazy people have children these days," says Professor Guardian. "Consequently children are increasingly stupid and lazy as well. In my opinion, educating the present generation is a complete waste of money."

The Portadown News 'Last Word'

"Democracy is the worst possible type of government, except all the others that have been tried" – *Sir Winston Churchill*

The Portadown News

18TH MAY 2001   www.PortadownNews.com

US FACT-FINDING MISSION

by our American correspondent, Brad Cheeseburger

ARIZONA Senator Mick O'Malley is back in Portadown for another election 'fact-finding' mission. Speaking to our reporter yesterday, the Senator outlined the facts he hopes to find.

"The main facts I plan to find concern British human rights abuses, RUC brutality, and harassment of Sinn Fein community representatives," he explained. "I may find some other facts, but those are the ones I'm really interested in."

Senator O'Malley has a long history of fact-finding in Northern Ireland. His previous discoveries include:

- Republican paramilitaries don't sell drugs
- RUC patrols regularly kill and eat children
- Queen Victoria personally ordered the potato famine

By complete coincidence Senator O'Malley is himself currently campaigning for re-election in Arizona, under the slogan: *"O'Malley Electrocutes More Blacks".*

COUNCIL UNVEILS TRANSPORT PLAN

The future of local transport was revealed yesterday with the publication of Craigavon Borough Council's "Transport 2020" plan. The £2-million consultant's report was compiled in the bar at the Silverwood Hotel, with additional input from hauliers, car dealers and people who own land near the motorway.

Its proposals cover five main areas:

CARS

The Council will lobby the Government to reclassify obesity as a disability. This will entitle most local women to a free car.

TRAINS

To prevent further disruption to rail services, the main line through Lurgan will be ripped up and sold to the gypsies. Passengers will be transferred between Moira and Portadown by army helicopter.

Kilwilkee Community Representative Brendan McAlinden has described the proposal as "a victory for common sense".

BUSES

To discourage stone-throwing, buses will no longer have windows. Drivers will navigate using GPS satellite equipment, while passengers will identify their stop by smell.

BICYCLES

To prevent fertility problems, all cyclists will be required to tie a pillow onto their saddle for any journey of more than 3 miles. To reduce punctures on the cycle path network, Buckfast will be sold only in plastic bottles.

CANALS

The canal network will be completely restored. This will allow local councillors to travel to tourism conferences.

'Acid bombs' were just the solution!

by our Drumcree correspondent, Will March

REPUBLICAN sources have explained the mysterious appearance of 'acid bombs' at Saturday's absolutely spontaneous and in no way pre-planned riot on the Garvaghy Road.

"It all started when one of our suppliers in England made a mistake with our weekly drug shipment," explained local community activist and Sinn Fein MLA Darren O'Hagan yesterday. "We'd ordered £100,000 of acid – and he apparently thought we meant **acid** acid. Imagine how we laughed when this container arrived full of plastic bottles marked 'caustic'."

However, the ever-resourceful Republicans soon turned the mistake to their advantage. "After having the people responsible shot and dumped in South Armagh, we put our heads together and came up with the 'acid bomb' concept," explained Mr O'Hagan. "It's been a great success, and just goes to show that whatever happens around here, it's always the RUC that gets it in the end."

EDITORIAL: is it time to withdraw from England?

Following last weekend's disgraceful race riots in Manchester, many British people are again asking if it is time to pull out of England. England consumes almost 85% of the national budget; we also have tens of thousands of troops stationed throughout the region. Yet still, the violence and chaos continues.

Fortunately people in Northern Ireland – unlike in any other part of the UK – are allowed to say who can remain British, and who gets forced into another jurisdiction regardless of international law. Once we've got rid of the English, we can turn our attention to other groups of people we don't like. Eventually the only people left in the country will be liberal, open-minded, educated young people like ourselves. You must all come over some evening for a glass of wine.

Can I have a job on The Guardian now? (The Editor)

NEW GOOD FRIDAY AGREEMENT UNVEILED!

by our politics correspondent, Jim Hacker

After extensive consultation with each other, the British and Irish governments have published an outline draft of The Good Friday Agreement Mark II, which will come into immediate effect should the current process fail.

Its main proposals are as follows:

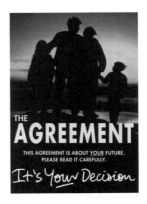

1. Northern Ireland will remain part of the United Kingdom forever.
2. England, Scotland and Wales will leave the United Kingdom.
3. The Irish Republic will join the United Kingdom.
4. The United Kingdom will be referred to as "Ireland".
5. Bertie Ahern will be crowned King.

"This is a great step forward for all the people of Northern Ireland," said Secretary of State Jock McThingy yesterday. "Now if you'll excuse me, I've got a plane to catch."

The Portadown News

www.PortadownNews.com

Mini 12th crowd 'ugliest ever'

by our Drumcree correspondent, Will March

According to security forces, the audience for last Saturday night's Mini 12th parade in Portadown was "the ugliest ever". Soldiers and police were nearly overcome with laughter, as hundreds of freaks, drunks, losers, retards, slappers and gits poured into town from wherever it is these people come from.

At one point, the RUC was forced to consider deploying water cannon due to a large concentration of smelly people at the top of West Street, but decided against it on medical advice.

The parade itself passed off peacefully, and was followed by a dignified religious service, a night of binge drinking and eight unplanned conceptions.

Anger at Navan closure

by our tourism correspondent, Johnny Foreigner

The magical, mystical atmosphere of Navan Fort must now be enjoyed without the benefit of a giftshop, following this week's closure of the site's £20-million Visitors' Centre.

"Armagh might as well forget about its tourist industry," said Navan Centre Manageress Nuala O'Tain yesterday. "It might have the best cinema and theatre outside Belfast, two ancient cathedrals, the planetarium and beautiful Georgian architecture – but unless visitors can walk round a small hill without a coffee shop nearby, then the whole local economy is basically shafted."

Meanwhile Dr Mick O'Riley, Professor of Celtic Racial Purity at Trinity, is warning that the closure of the Navan Centre brings a wider threat to society. "The numerous 'Visitors' Centres' that have sprung up around Ireland North and South over the past few years are vital in maintaining a strong Irish Celtic identity," explains the Professor in his latest paper, 'Fuck Off Britannia: A Cross-Community Approach to Peacemaking'.

"If people can't obtain a view of Irish history through anodyne, third-rate audio-visual displays such as those at the Navan Centre, they might go to their local library or bookshop for information instead," says the Professor. "Then they'd find out that Irish and British culture have been inextricably linked for thousands of years, which would leave me looking like a complete arsehole."

6 THE PORTADOWN NEWS

NORTHWAY SCHEME TO CHANGE OUR LIVES

by our development correspondent, Des Res

After years of consultation, planning and bribery, the Northway improvement scheme has finally begun. The project will upgrade a 500-metre stretch of the Northway from two to four lanes, cutting three seconds off the journey between the traffic jam on the Armagh Road and the new traffic jam it will create at Seagoe.

The new scheme will also include an off-ramp to the Vico Developments 'retail park' at the old gasworks site in Edenderry. This new shopping mecca will comprise a row of tin sheds slowly rusting and filling up with toxic fumes, where teenagers on minimum wage will scowl at you while you browse the same selection of sweatshop-produced crap already available three miles up the road at Craigavon.

"It's true that for the next six months, while awaiting these many fantastic benefits, Portadown's commuters will end every working day inching back down the Northway like lobotomised lemmings, staring at some twat's 'No Fear' sticker while suffocating in their own filth," admits Department of Regional Development spokesman Terry McAdam. "Still if you've got a problem with global capitalism you can always vote for the Workers Party. Now fuck off."

BELFAST RIOTING: "TUT TUT", SAYS PORTADOWN

by our paramilitary correspondent, P. O'Neill

Portadown's Protestant and non-Protestant residents were united in horror this week at the disgraceful rioting in North Belfast. The trouble was initially orchestrated by a group of primary school children, and quickly escalated despite UDA and Sinn Fein attempts to calm the situation.

"Obviously our hearts go out to the people of the Ardoyne," said Craigavon Mayor Ed Hawke yesterday. "On the other hand, this does mean that next time some arrogant Belfast fucker gives you a dirty look because of where you come from, you can point up at the Cave Hill and laugh in his face."

EDITORIAL: the price of peace

A shock report last week revealed that policing the Drumcree dispute over the past six years has cost £1 billion – equivalent to £50,000 for every man, woman and child in Portadown. Few people, on hearing this horrifying statistic, could fail to think, "That's enough money to get me out of this miserable hole." Hence the Portadown News, on behalf – we believe – of all the decent people of Portadown, urges the Government to let the angryheads knock seven bells out of each other, and give the rest of us a nice fat cheque.

Alice Mothball

In Memoriam

Another life wasted in church

The death has taken place of Ms Alice Mothball, the well-known and liked local spinster. Born in 1912, Ms Mothball was a lifelong member of Tandragee Road Unreconstructed Presbyterian, where members of the congregation paid tribute yesterday to her many years of service.

"Alice made a huge contribution to the church," said fellow old lady Violet Bluerinse. "She dutifully turned up every Sunday, even after it was obvious she'd never meet a man. As the years dragged on and the loneliness began to eat away at her soul, her enthusiasm for tent missions and even car boot sales became truly inspirational."

Minister Brian Blackhead also paid tribute to Ms Mothball's life of sacrifice. "You know I don't think Alice ever even had a proper orgasm," said Mr Blackhead. "Ironic, really, considering how much she loved playing the organ."

RUC REFORM MAY DESTROY HOUSING MARKET – CLAIM

by our housing correspondent, Des Res
Leading local estate agents William Joyce have claimed that RUC reform will devastate the housing market in Portadown's outlying villages.

"Who's going to spend £100K on a cheesy prefab box in Tandragee or Richhill once the RUC has gone?" asked sales manager Noel Roderick yesterday. "New RUC officers had loads of money, no sense, total paranoia and stuck-up girlfriends. You could flog a whole development in an afternoon. God, I'm going to miss those guys."

However such pessimism may be premature. When our reporter pointed out that pretty much the same kind of people would be applying for posts in the new Northern Ireland Police Service, Mr Roderick cheered up immediately. "Of course, you're right," he said. "I don't know what I got so worked up about."

New terrorist organisation launched

by our paramilitary correspondent, P. O'Neill
NORTHERN IRELAND has a brand new terrorist organisation today, with the official launch in Lurgan of the 38-County Sovereignty Committee. The new terror group aims for a united socialist republic consisting of all 32 counties in Ireland, plus six counties in England where Irish people may be in the majority.

At a star-studded gala press launch yesterday, Lurgan terror chief Brendan McAlinden explained his new group's 'analysis' of the political situation.

"I think we all realise that the English want nothing more to do with Ireland," said Mr McAlinden. "What's less well known is that there are large parts of England they're not too keen on either. In fact, basically anything north of Peterborough is up for grabs."

The 38-County Sovereignty Committee opens for business this evening, with a hoax bomb on the railway line at Kilwilkee followed by a community stoning of the bomb squad. Later tonight, any teenagers who did not participate in the rioting will be shot in the legs for antisocial behaviour.

"There's no doubt about it," said Mr McAlinden. "These are exciting times to be a republican!"

Five more inquiries planned

by our security correspondent, Roger Base

In a surprise move last night, Canadian judge Peter Cory has recommended a further five inquiries into suspicious deaths in Northern Ireland:

Jane Kennedy
Disappeared April 2004. British government may be responsible.

Shergar
Equine rights lawyer, last seen entering Dundalk kebab shop.

Jeffrey Donaldson's leadership bid
Definite suicide, but David Burnside may have questions to answer.

Maysfield Leisure Centre
Killed during row over money. Belfast City Council accused of collusion.

1,854 IRA victims (and counting)
Securocrat-backed media conspiracy to undermine the peace process.

DICK ON THE BOX
Tonight's TV, with Dick McDonald

6:00–6:30 Police Six
Stolen property news, screened just after you get back from Nutts Corner.
Starring a nervous-looking policeman.

6:30–7:00 Local News
Another firebombed family begs for peace from their hideous sofa.
Followed by Shit Weather.

7:00–7:30 School Up My Arse

Frank Mitchell invites more local children to visit the school up his arse.
Parental Advisory: Features arsehole.

7:30–8:30 Awash with Colour
Another beautiful Ulster landscape is captured on canvas, before some fucker builds a bungalow on it.

8.30–9.30 Town Challenge
Desperate attempt to devise some form of sporting competition that doesn't have sectarian overtones.
This week: Crossmaglen vs. Ballymena.

9:30–10:00 Give Us Some Credit
More harmless 'troubles' humour as two families with serious paramilitary involvement somehow get through the day without sinking into a mire of pointless hatred.
Starring The Whole Lot of Shite Gang.

10:00–11:00 Spotlight
Investigating claims that a bunch of arrogant wankers from the London dinner-party circuit have conspired to steal £120 a year off every household in the country.
Warning: Your address is on the computer.

11:00–12:00 Kelly
Psychic superstar Mystic Meg summons the spirit of philosopher John Stuart Mill, while the studio audience discusses the role of the social contract in conflict resolution.
Plus a new song from Jason Donovan.

12:00–12:03 Closedown
Where they used to play the National Anthem, before the fenians ruined it for everybody.

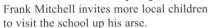

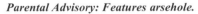

NORTHWAY CRISIS LOOMS

by our development correspondent, Des Res

The Northway upgrade scheme is in disarray tonight after Obins Street residents launched a last-minute planning objection. "This road is clearly designed to intimidate local people," claims Concerned Residents Obins Street Section (C.R.O.S.S.) Chairperson Aideen O'Rourke. "Many of the cars using the road will be BMWs, which is blatant triumphalism."

However the Department of Regional Development has hit back, insisting that the Northway follow its traditional route. Popular South African mediator Brian Currin has now been called in to chair proximity talks. The following compromise positions are on the table:

1. Cars switch off their engines and coast through the disputed section.
2. A tunnel is built under The Tunnel, to be known as "The Tunnel Tunnel".
3. Commuters receive permission to use the Northway, but phone in sick.
4. England takes back its money and says, "Fuck you all."

"I did also suggest that people just take the train to Belfast," Mr Currin told our reporter yesterday, "But everybody laughed at me."

CHRISTIANS DO THEIR PART

by our religion correspondent, Helen Brimstone

A series of 'prayer workshops' has been organised by the town's main churches in the run-up to the marching season. "Prayer has a fantastic track record throughout human history in the prevention of violence, war, famine and disease," explained Rev. Brian Blackhead of Tandragee Road Unreconstructed Presbyterian yesterday. "We're confident that by sitting about talking to ourselves and feeling smug we can ensure a peaceful July for all the people of Portadown."

NEW Peace Wall Proposed

by our security correspondent, Roger Base

Following last week's rioting at the Edgarstown bonfire, the Portadown News can exclusively reveal that plans are being considered to extend the Charles Street peace wall.

The new wall will run south from Maghery to Richill, then east to Lurgan via Bleary, and north to Kinnego.

A further wall from Kinnego back to Maghery along the Lough Neagh shore is also being reviewed, pending an inquiry into how many local people own boats.

"Peace walls are a regrettable necessity," said Secretary of State Jock McThingy yesterday. "However some peace walls are less regrettable than others."

LOCAL ORANGEMEN ARRESTED IN BOLIVIA

by our Peace Process correspondent, Phil O'Buster

Security forces in Bolivia have arrested three leading Portadown Orangemen. David Jones (52), David Burrows (35) and Harold Gracey (75) have been charged under the South American country's notorious Acto par Preventio de Terrorismo, and have been transferred to the dreaded Our Blessed Virgin of the Andes maximum security prison.

The British ambassador to Bolivia, Sir Andy Hill, met the three men this morning but was unable to explain why they had been arrested.

"It's a bit of a mystery," Sir Andy told reporters this morning. "They just kept saying 'Where's the marching powder? Where's the marching powder?', over and over again."

Indian Chief returns home

by our American correspondent, Brad Cheeseburger

Sioux medicine man Big Chief Falling Water has left Portadown after his most successful series of rain dances to date. Every July the RUC invites Big Chief Falling Water to visit the town and summon up bad weather.

"Rioting is a completely weather-related phenomenon," explained RUC constable Bill Mason yesterday. "If the sun's shining, every dickhead in town is out looking a fight. When it's raining, they sit inside watching 'Xena: Warrior Princess' and eating chips."

Big Chief Falling Water is delighted with the success of his visit, and hopes for lasting peace in Northern Ireland. "For obvious reasons," he explained yesterday, "we really don't want any more Irish people coming to America."

Summer evacuation 'makes Portadown dumber and fatter'

by our social affairs correspondent, Grant Dole

New monthly figures from the DSS indicate that during July, the average citizen of Portadown suffers a 38-point fall in IQ and a 3-stone increase in weight. The shock figures are being blamed on the annual Drumcree exodus, when anyone with any sense leaves town, taking all the attractive women with them.

"Obviously these are average figures," explained DSS statistician Orla Harrigan. "The only way an individual would suffer such an IQ drop and weight gain in a single month would be to eat chips continuously while banging their head against a wall, which rarely happens outside Edgarstown."

Drumcree

www.PortadownNews.com

PARKING DISPUTE GETS NASTY

Two Portadown men have become embroiled in a bitter neighbourhood parking dispute, it emerged this week. Mr Seamus Green has made a series of demands over the past seven years that next-door-neighbour Mr Billy March stop parking his car outside his house.

"I've lived in this house for 30 years," Mr Green said yesterday, "and I always park my car right outside. It's my traditional parking space." But Mr March hit back. "My car's taxed, so I have the right to park it wherever I like," he said. "Mr Green can park his car outside my house if it really bothers him that much."

When we put this to Mr Green, he agreed that everyone has the right to park outside his house, but questioned Mr March's motives for doing so. "Whatever he says about laws and rights, the fact is I know he does it just to annoy me," said Mr Green.

The Portadown News contacted popular South African mediator Brian Currin to see if he could help resolve the parking impasse. "Oh for Christ's sake," said Mr Currin yesterday, "you people are worse than the blacks."

QUEEN, POPE APPEAL FOR VIOLENCE

by our Drumcree correspondent, Will March

Queen Elizabeth and Pope John Paul have both appealed for violence at this year's Drumcree parade. "The politics of the 16th century remain close to our heart," said Queen Elizabeth in a statement yesterday. "We urge all our loyal subjects in Portadown to remember their history by endlessly repeating it as violently as possible."

Meanwhile the Pope has offered a personal message of support to Garvaghy Road Residents Spokesman Brendan McKenna.

"As far as this issue is concerned," said the ailing pontiff yesterday, "Christ's message is 'bomb your neighbour'."

Councillor Jones gets to work

by our politics correspondent, Jim Hacker

Newly-elected councillor David Jones has denied that his Orange Order links will jeopardise the local economy. "I am not a single-issue candidate, and will treat all my official engagements with the sensitivity expected of a true Son of Orange," said Mr Jones, speaking at a European investment conference in the Civic Centre this morning.

He then presented the German delegate with a video of "The Dambusters", and goose-stepped across the car park.

Stop Press: Drumcree breakthrough rumoured

There are rumours of an early solution to the Drumcree crisis today after it emerged that Harold Gracey has booked a fortnight for two to Ibiza departing July 14th.

When advised by our reporter that Ibiza is full of pill-popping clubbers, Mr Gracey replied, "Everybody else takes drugs, so why shouldn't I?"

The Portadown News

17TH AUGUST 2001   www.PortadownNews.com

Portadown Grammar exam results 'best ever'

by our education correspondent, Una O'Level

Portadown Grammar has announced its best exam results ever, thanks to the usual combination of threats, expulsions, bribery and downright dishonesty.

"Middle-class parents expect exam results to improve every year," explained Headmaster Tom Flannel to our reporter yesterday. "However, human intelligence can only increase over an evolutionary timespan. Consequently, I have no choice but to cheat like a bastard."

Following this year's record-breaking 105% pass-rate, Mr Flannel hopes Portadown Grammar will be listed in The Sunday Times Top 10 Shitty Little Provincial Grammar Schools That Think They're The Business. "Of course," he admits, "this means we'll have to fiddle the rugby results as well."

Everyone welcome at West Portadown Festival

by our Irish culture correspondent, A. Mone

Organisers of this weekend's West Portadown Festival have denied claims that the event is a Sinn Fein stunt.

"This is a celebration for the whole community," claimed Festival Brigade Commander Darren O'Hagan yesterday. "Just because you're a fucking Prod doesn't mean you can't enjoy Christy Moore."

"We've also got the Wolfe Tones," added Festival Quartermaster Brendan McKenna, "and Wolfe Tone was a fucking Prod, as you'd know if they taught proper history in those heathen schools of yours."

Riverfront plans unveiled

by our development correspondent, Des Res

The Planning Office has unveiled its proposal for the long-overdue development of Portadown's riverfront. Commenting on the plans, a Craigavon Borough Council spokesman said, "Consume, reproduce, die; Consume, reproduce, die."

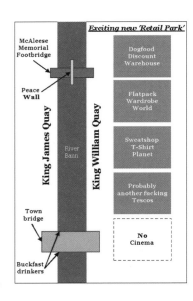

Exciting new 'Retail Park'

McAleese Memorial Footbridge

Peace Wall

King James Quay

King William Quay

River Bann

Town bridge

Buckfast drinkers

Dogfood Discount Warehouse

Flatpack Wardrobe World

Sweatshop T-Shirt Planet

Probably another fucking Tescos

No Cinema

3,000 found dead

**by our paramilitary correspondent,
P. O'Neill**

Northern Ireland is in shock today after the discovery of 3,000 bodies at various locations around the country.

"It's too early to say who is responsible," RUC Officer Bill Mason told a packed press conference yesterday, "however we believe the cause of death to be a lethal cocktail of religion and politics."

Local youth worker Grant McDonald has urged parents to remain calm.

"Many young people in Northern Ireland do experiment with religion and politics," explained Mr McDonald. "Fortunately, the vast majority of them are far too stoned to let it ruin their lives."

SINN FEIN DENIES COLOMBIAN CONNECTION

RUC to scrap Rule 21

**by our policing correspondent,
Roz Peeler**

The RUC is considering the abolition of its controversial Rule 21, which bars members of Crown forces from using hurling sticks to beat up children.

"For historical reasons, the use of hurling sticks has been unacceptable to many in the RUC," Portadown-based officer Bill Mason told our reporter yesterday. "We didn't want ourselves associated with a bunch of backward inbred muck-savages hanging around freezing concrete buildings in the middle of nowhere listening to Christy Moore tapes and taking collections for the IRA."

"However," added PC Mason, "we have to recognise the progress hurling has made towards becoming a normal sport that can win the respect of the wider community. Though I still prefer the ice hockey myself, to be honest."

NEW HOPE FOR PEACE AS INSTITUTIONS REOPEN

by our education correspondent, Una O'Level

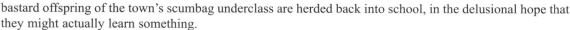

With the end of the school holidays, an air of quiet satisfaction hangs over Portadown. Law-abiding citizens are looking forward to fairly quiet evenings and slightly less dangerous weekends, as the bastard offspring of the town's scumbag underclass are herded back into school, in the delusional hope that they might actually learn something.

"Actually, I don't know why people look forward to the start of term," Clounagh High School Headmaster A.N. Sickdon told our reporter yesterday. "They must have forgotten that September is the start of the firework season."

Portadown Poundstretcher "Saddest place on Earth"

by our retail correspondent, Kaye Mart

A United Nations survey has declared Portadown's Poundstretcher store "The saddest place on Earth", heading off strong competition from Bangladesh, Chad and Strabane.

The international team of inspectors was impressed with the store's shabby appearance, worthless stock, demeaning service and 'interesting' smell, but have stressed that it was the people of Portadown itself who made the crucial difference.

"They brilliantly capture the futility of consumerism," explained UN statistician Kim-Song Ahmed Mbeki. "Despite having no money to spare, they still have to acquire pointless bits of plastic crap to feel they belong to society. Although I've got to admit, the batteries are a bargain."

The happiest place on Earth is Disneyworld.

Sociologist welcomes Ardoyne protest

by our welfare correspondent, Grant Dole

Penny O'Guardian, Portadown's leading sociologist, claims the Ardoyne school crisis may be a positive development for Northern Ireland.

"Thanks to this protest, a whole generation of parents is learning to get up in the morning," she told our reporter yesterday. "As recently as June, few people in North Belfast ever saw 8 a.m. – unless they'd been up all night, anyway. Now all that has changed forever. By discovering, as a community, that it is actually possible to get up regularly at a decent hour, they are taking their first vital steps towards self-respect."

On Dr O'Guardian's advice, the Department of Social Security has printed a leaflet for those inspired by the Spirit of Ardoyne: *'So You've Finally Got Up Before Lunchtime'* is available now from the Jobcentre.

IRA HIJACK HORROR

by our security correspondent, Roger Base

Portadown residents watched in horror yesterday as a microlight crashed into Magowan Buildings.

The twin-cylinder aircraft had earlier been hijacked from Mullahead Road Microlight Training School by crazed IRA terrorists, brandishing potato peelers and shouting, "Gerry is Great!"

The microlight's pilot spoke to his wife moments before impact by mobile telephone; she described him as sounding, "Like a man shouting over a lawnmower in a strong wind." Dozens of people believed to be in Magowan Buildings at the time of the crash are still missing. Police are searching the DSS, Gary's Bar and underneath the town bridge. The attack will also have serious long-term implications for the Portadown's vital shoe repair and knock-off clothing industries.

Speaking to reporters after an emergency cabinet meeting today, Prime Minister Tony Blair urged the people of Portadown to remain calm in the face of catastrophe.

"As far as Northern Ireland is concerned, we are now at peace with terrorism, actually," he said, "So let's get back to moving forward, OK?"

City status for Craigavon

After extensive consultation throughout Portadown Golf Club, the Borough Council has decided to apply for city status for Craigavon.

To qualify for city status, a town must have the following amenities:

1. Affordable drugs
2. Lots of roundabouts
3. A big lake full of shit
4. Sainsburys

The main advantage of city status is that it will allow us to tell those pretentious wankers in Armagh to go fuck themselves.

If you would like to congratulate us on our latest ingenious scheme to waste your money, please write to:

Trevor Cloudy, City Manager, City Hall, Craigavon City Centre, Craigavon City.

Editorial: Let's Get Even

Following this week's terrible outrage, there can be no doubt that the people of Portadown are At War With Terrorism. Everything must be done to capture the evil mastermind behind this atrocity, and make him pay for his diabolical crime.

Possibly by appointing him Minister for Education.

The Portadown News

1ST OCTOBER 2001

www.PortadownNews.com

Tandragee Road, Portadown

Application to cut down trees, drain meadows and construct hundreds of nasty little plywood houses six inches apart and three miles from the nearest shop. Houses to be sold for £90K minimum, trapping their guillible buyers into a lifetime of debt and loveless marriages, and all for what? To put a roof over their stupid heads in a little provincial town where house prices have tripled in five years but wages have hardly kept pace with inflation.

Outline approval also requested to build a retail park should the houses be completely destroyed in a massive flood caused by this pointless and half-arsed drainage of the town's entire upstream flood plain.

NORTHWAY ROADWORKS: TRAFFIC UPDATE

Phase 1 of the Northway upgrade scheme ("Cutting down trees and driving JCBs around at 5mph in rush hour") is complete. Phase 2 ("Closing the Bann Bridge for ten months and drinking tea") commences this weekend.

The following alternative arrangements have been made for commuters needing to cross the river between now and next June:

7am–10am, Mon–Fri
Temporary Pontoon bridge, Maghery.
Toll £15.

10am–4pm, Mon–Fri
Diversion via Spelga Dam.

4pm–8pm, Mon–Fri
Chinook heli-lifter service, Fee £2,500.

8pm–7am, Mon–Fri
Amphibious vehicles only.

Weekends and bank holidays
Build your own raft. Materials for sale from the site office.

Emergencies
Ask Citizens Advice Bureau for information on "railway trains".

PIG FARMERS DEMAND COMPENSATION FOR RISE OF ISLAM

by our agriculture correspondent, Culchie McMucker

The Northern Ireland Farmers Union has expressed its members' concerns about the conflict in Afghanistan.

"Ultimately, this is a struggle between capitalist liberal democracy and the reactionary forces of theocratic absolutism," explained NIFU local chairman Josias Bogman, while standing in some shit outside a barn in Annaghmore yesterday. "Should Islam triumph, there will be serious implications for world-wide pork consumption, and we'll be demanding compensation."

Mr Bogman wants the European Union to set up a $10-billion contingency fund.

"If a global imposition of Sharia law makes consuming our product punishable by death, obviously we'll still have to continue farming," added Mr Bogman. "After all, we've been producing crap nobody eats for years, and I don't see why the collapse of Western civilisation should make any difference. Now get off my land."

Confusion over 'War on Terrorism'

by our security correspondent, Roger Base

Downing Street has been forced to issue a series of embarrassing clarifications following its recent declaration of a "War on Terrorism".

After realising that this would mean shooting Gerry Adams, Number Ten quickly declared the UK to be at war strictly with "international terrorism".

After further realising that the IRA operates in Ireland and Britain, Number Ten then declared the UK to be only at war with "Terrorism operating across unanimously agreed national territories".

After additionally realising that the IRA has operated in Holland, Germany and Gibraltar ('The Occupied Six Acres'), Number Ten declared the UK to be at war with "intercontinental terrorism".

Finally, after realising that the IRA is still active in Cuba, Libya and Colombia, Number Ten has declared the UK to be at war with terrorism, "when it suits us".

Local Muslims feel more at home

by our religious affairs correspondent, Helen Brimstone

Portadown's small Muslim community believes that the September 11th attacks in New York have actually benefited community relations in the town.

"I think we're finally starting to relate to the native Portadown people," explained Iman Ali Akhbar Rafsanjanibashtar yesterday. "After all, now everybody thinks we're a bunch of murdering religious fanatics as well."

"Cross Words"

The Portadown News Church Column

This week: Pastor Clifford Morrison explains why Baptists can park anywhere they like.

Unsaved people often say to me: "Pastor Morrison, how come so many members of your congregation insist on blocking the Meadow Lane bypass with their flash cars, even though you've a perfectly good car-park sitting half-empty right behind the church?"

The answer to this question, like all questions, is of course to be found in The Scriptures:

When thou seekest to
praise The Lord
Gather about thee thy
earthly family
In their nice hats
And place them in thy new
wagon
Which thou hast washed
And driveth it unto the
very gates of the House
of The Lord

Hypocrites 6.6.6

New-look IRA unveiled

by our paramilitary correspondent, P. O'Neill

As part of its commitments under the Good Friday Agreement, the IRA will be relaunched next week as The Northern Ireland Terrorist Service (N.I.T.S.).

"From now on, the IRA will aim to work with Loyalist drug dealers and racketeers, under the slogan 'Towards a true reflection of the criminal element'," explained Martin McGuinness yesterday. Mr McGuinness, who was not the leader of the IRA, is hotly tipped for the position of not the leader of the N.I.T.S.

While only the most horrible of Unionists would dispute that real progress has been made, some issues remain unresolved, in particular the question of the Terrorist Service's new uniform. The traditional balaclava is considered 'offensive' by many people who have been shot, but the current alternative – a turban – may also convey negative symbolism.

GAA to be partitioned

by our sports correspondent, A. Bore

As controversy continues to rage over Rule 21, GAA chiefs have come up with a radical solution that will hopefully accommodate both sides.

The six north-eastern counties which continually refuse to agree with the rest of the island will be organised into a separate association, to be known as Northern GAA.

"As the 'Yes' and 'No' camps will never agree, we'll just give the 'No' people their own little Association," explained GAA Grand Wizard Brendan O'Mucksavage yesterday. "Then the rest of us can forget all about them, and get on with our lives in peace."

Journey beyond your imagination.

Harry Potter
and the Wicked Witch

Not denounced from the pulpit

CIGARETTE HAUL 'FOR PERSONAL USE'

by our crime correspondent, Rob Berry

The Real IRA has claimed the cigarette shipment seized in Warrenpoint last month was 'for personal use'. The record-breaking £50 million haul was impounded by customs officials, however they may now have to be returned under European Union free trade rules.

The Real IRA's claims have been backed up by prominent Dundalk republican Rory O'Splitter. "Apparently the Real IRA was planning to have a big party," he said yesterday, "although in the end nobody showed up."

Flags issue solved!

by our symbolism correspondent, Meta F. Orr

Craigavon Borough Council has resolved the divisive flags issue with a new design that reflects all sections of the community.

"The Red Finger of Ulster" (*pictured*) features the traditional red hand on a white background, with middle finger rampant.

It was designed by a committee of councillors, design students, management consultants, and some woman from the Arts Council. An advertising campaign will take place encouraging people to use the new flag, featuring the slogan: 'Craigavon – fly the finger'.

"We had originally hoped to use a design submitted by local schoolchildren," DUP Councillor Marvin Currie explained yesterday. "Unfortunately, they were all shite."

The Portadown News

2001   www.PortadownNews.com

Portadown to have own spaceport
by our development correspondent, Des Res

Portadown will soon have its first spaceport, according to local development agency Portadown 2000. A presentation was delivered on the exciting development in the town hall yesterday, complete with an artist's impression of the spaceport and a scale model of the alien quarantine centre proposed for Ballyoran.

"The essence of town planning is to always think of the future," explained flamboyant local architect and Portadown 2000 representative Sam Weird. "As we can see from watching TV programmes such as 'Star Trek' and 'Babylon 5', at some point in the future space travel will be routine, with people travelling instantly between planets using either 'Warp Drive' or 'Jump Gates'."

"When this happens, only towns with their own spaceport can expect to continue attracting the sort of investment that Portadown needs to live long and prosper."

Asked when Portadown could expect to have a cinema, Mr Weird replied, "Well, now you're just being silly."

Council demands protection money from stallholders
by our paramilitary correspondent, P. O'Neill

The RUC is investigating claims that Craigavon Borough Council Chief Executive Terrence Cloudy is demanding protection money from Portadown's market traders.

Initial complaints were received last week from popular clothing retailer and long-time Brownstown resident Mr Mohammed Ali Akbar Rafsanjani. "I was minding my own business – literally – in front of St Mark's last Saturday afternoon, when suddenly Mr Cloudy appeared beside the stall and started menacing me," Mr Rafsanjani told our reporter yesterday. "He brandished a court order and said 'Give me all your takings, or I'll have you on the first banana-boat back to Pakistan.'"

"Obviously I was terrified," continued Mr Rafsanjani, "as I am actually from India."

According to witnesses, Mr Cloudy then pocketed the contents of Mr Rafsanjani's cash-drawer, and made off in the direction of Jameson's.

Other stall-holders refused to speak publicly about the incident, but one told us anonymously that Mr Cloudy's protection demands have been going on for months. "Everything Mohammed says is true, but the rest of us are too frightened to speak out," she whispered. "If we go public, the bastard will have us all rate-capped."

Lookalikes

UUP's Dr Esmond Birnie in 'Mars Attacks' shock

Hugh Orde in Pearse McAuley shock

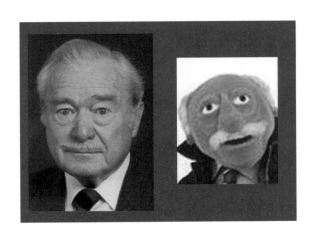

UUP's Sir John Gorman in 'Waldorf' from The Muppets shock

Sinn Fein's Barry McElduff in 'Radar' from M*A*S*H shock

Our Wee Jeffrey

www.PortadownNews.com

Donaldson demands further proof

by our religion correspondent, Helen Brimstone

Renegade Ulster Unionist MP Jeffrey Donaldson (5'2") has shocked party colleagues by denouncing Christianity.

"I have read The Bible in full, and I'm afraid that I am not impressed," Mr Donaldson told our reporter yesterday. "After all that humanity has suffered, this very vague document will not satisfy my requirements for eternal peace."

"I am a modest man," added Mr Donaldson. "But should God fail to prove his existence before February, I may have to call upon myself to rule the universe."

CRIMESTOPPERS

A man walked into the Ulster Unionist Council meeting last Saturday, issued a series of demands, and made off with a small quantity of votes. He is 4'2", lightweight and speaks with a strong Lisburn accent. If you know of his whereabouts, please phone Crimestoppers immediately.

'UNITED I STAND' – DONALDSON

by our unionist correspondent, William Splitter

A campaign for unionist unity has been launched by everyone who thinks they're about to be kicked out of the Ulster Unionist Party.

'Unionists should stick together,' said Jeffrey Donaldson yesterday, 'otherwise there's no chance of getting rid of David Trimble.'

'We hope our new initiative will unite the unionist family,' added David Burnside while clearing his desk this morning. 'Now if you'll excuse me, I've got to phone Peter Robinson.'

What next for Jeffrey?

by our unionist correspondent, Will March

The Portadown News has obtained this purported draft copy of Jeffrey Donaldson's resignation letter.

Dear David

Following Monday's Ulster Unionist Council vote I have been reluctantly forced to reconsider my ~~ambition~~ position. I cannot stand idly by while the government makes concessions to ~~you~~ terrorists, nor can I bear to see the country I love ruled by ~~you~~ Dublin. Consequently I have decided to ~~hang around for years causing trouble~~ resign.

Yours sincerely
Jeffrey Donaldson, Party ~~Leader~~ Member

Jeffrey caught short

by our Westminster correspondent, Bill Pending

5ft

Despite failing to follow through with his threatened resignation, supporters are denying claims that Jeffrey Donaldson is 'the Clare Short of the Ulster Unionist Party'.

'It's true that Jeffrey is short,' conceded a spokesman yesterday, 'but that's as far as it goes.'

LEAVE IT OUT JEFFREY

by our refuse correspondent, Chorlton Wheeliebin

Lisburn City Council has reminded Jeffrey Donaldson to put his bin out.

'It's no use just leaving the back door ajar,' warned a council official yesterday. 'We're not taking any more of his rubbish until it's all out in the open.'

What in God's name am I doing with my little life?

Powerless to Change

I have resigned . . . myself to yet more emergency meetings

Local woman has a child, you know

by our social affairs correspondent, Grant Dole

Craigavon Magistrates Court has dropped a shoplifting charge against Portadown woman Kelly-Anne Jervis (19) after she delivered a moving appeal for clemency.

"I have a child, you know," said Miss Jervis. Amid gasps of respect from the public gallery, Magistrate Ken Dixon ordered her immediate and unconditional release.

"I am shocked by this outrageous injustice against a mother," Mr Dixon told the court, "and also hugely impressed by your ability to reproduce. You are free to go."

Summing up, Mr Dixon described arresting officer Bill Mason as "clearly a heartless bastard". The plaintiff, Portadown High Fashions, was fined £5,000 for wasting maternal time.

HUNGER STRIKE FEAR

by our security correspondent, Roger Base

The Police Service has expressed concern that a hunger strike by Holy Cross parents may considerably prolong the crisis.

"The typical hunger strike is over in about six months," PSNI Officer Bill Mason told our reporter yesterday. "However the average North Belfast resident has enough fat reserves to survive for up to two years."

MEADOW LANE ROADWORKS SAVED FOR THE NATION

by our motoring correspondent, Fred Petrolhead

The historic roadworks at Meadow Lane have been acquired by the National Trust.

"We have obtained a preservation order, enabling us to maintain this essential part of Portadown's character for future generations," explained National Trust spokesperson Rusty Castle yesterday.

The National Trust decided to act after reports that Tesco contractors had moved traffic cones on at least two occasions over the past year.

"That kind of vandalism shows no respect for our heritage," added Mr Castle. "Portadown without the Meadow Lane roadworks would be like Paris without springtime."

Property Page

45 Ballyhannon Parade

Identical to Curtingdon Grove, but £30,000 more expensive.

It's not Killicomaine, honest.

999 Copse Manor, Tandragee

Walled garden, secure parking, triple glazing, steel-reinforced doors, strategic elevation.

Special deal arranged with Patton Removals.

1690 Jervis Street

An ideal property for a single person or young couple who like trains, band parades, ignorant children, and the sound a Vauxhall Corsa makes hitting speed-bumps at 70mph.

Your home is at risk if you do not put a flag out.

100 Century Street

A delightful location beside Edenvilla Park, convenient to all amenities.

On-street parking not recommended.

69 Curtingdon Grove

Custom-assembled from plywood to your demanding specifications. Includes luxury fitted catflap, strange little room you'll never use, and bathroom fittings that looked a bit kinky in the brochure, but turn out to be barely big enough for one.

Stupid couples only.

"Dunmarchin", Ulsterville Avenue

Extensively renovated former Executive property. Features stained glass 'Harold Gracey' bathroom window, car port with fitted mini-bar, tragically inappropriate conservatory, and enormous white bedroom wardrobes that you'll not get out without taking the roof off.

Ground rent includes arch storage fee.

"The Bungalow", Annaghmore

Enjoy the view this house ruins for everyone else. Includes hideous outbuildings, and front garden full of weird stuff like old phone boxes and bits of traction engines.

Surveyor's note: load-bearing pebbledash.

Christmas

2001 | www.PortadownNews.com

New!
Identikit

No more 'looking different' terror!

INDENTIKIT clothing offers an extensive range of absolutely identical sportswear for the unfit gentleman.

This Christmas, give the Portadown Man in your life what he really wants – absolute conformity.

Lurgan Christmas Appeal

by our Lurgan correspondent, Sam 'Spade' McGrath

At this special time of year, our thoughts turn to those less fortunate than ourselves. In the spirit of the season, The Portadown News is proud to launch this year's Lurgan Christmas Appeal.

Everyday life in Lurgan is a struggle that we to the West can hardly imagine. Women must travel great distances to acquire essential domestic items, while children as young as 10 are often sent out to work in the pharmaceutical industry. Many things which we take for granted are unavailable, particularly soap, shampoo, toothpaste, deodorant and washing powder.

Please give generously. Lurgan's tragedy has already created a terrible refugee problem in Moira, and if the situation isn't controlled, they might start moving here as well.

Fidoway Dog Composter

 =

The Perfect Christmas Gift!

There's no more unwanted pet misery with the Fidoway Handy Garden Dog Composter. Simply kill the animal, place its carcass in the stylish Fidoway unit, wait three months – and spread evenly.

As seen on "Vets in Practice"

"The men behind the wire"

Customer Notice

Traditional Christmas Power Cuts

If your power goes off this Christmas, please note the following:

- Mankind survived for 2.5 million years without electricity.
- A week won't kill you.
- Calling the hotline makes no difference.
- Look, are you really going to complain about your turkey thawing out while 7 million Afghans are starving?
- There's nothing on TV anyway.
- Northern Ireland has the most expensive electricity in Europe: just imagine how much money you're saving.
- If you think we're useless, wait until they privatise the Water Service.

Christmas Shopping in Tandragee

A Portadown News Advertising Feature

As Christmas approaches, you may want to venture off the beaten track a little for those more unusual gift ideas. *There, how's that for an introduction? Sure beats – 'Shopping in the Sticks', eh?*

Just five miles away, Tandragee offers many surprises to the Portadown shopper. *Yeah, like 'Why are all these buildings lying empty?' and 'What the fuck is that smell?'*

Have you ever considered, for example, buying a new extractor fan for Christmas? *No, of course not. But Tandragee Extractor Fans have bought an advertisement in this stupid feature, so I have to write about them anyway.* Yes! Whisk those unpleasant turkey-cooking odours away with a new fan from Tandragee Extractor Fans!

Of course no Christmas dinner is complete without a massive attack of indigestion, which is why a visit to Tandragee Chemist's Shop is essential.

They stock a wide range of anti-acid tablets to help you through the Queen's Speech with minimum discomfort. *Just don't ask for contraception, or they'll start waving their fucking Bibles at you.*

Finally, after completing your Christmas shopping in Tandragee's relaxed rural charm, don't forget to stop at Wong's Tandragee Temple for a festive feast of Sweet & Sour Pork Noodles! *Right, there's another piece of cutting-edge local journalism ready for publication. I'm off to Bennett's to get wasted.*

Christmas

It's the toy every kid wants this Christmas!!!!

NEW!
Harry Potter puberty doll
Pus-shooting zits!
Moody spells!
Unpredictable wand!

CHRISTMAS SHOPPING IN BUSTLING PORTADOWN

A Portadown News advertising feature

Discerning shoppers will find all they need this Christmas in bustling Portadown. The town's many charity shops, famous for their 'old lady' smell, have a wide selection of affordable gift items ideal for relatives you don't really like. For book-worms, there's a choice of four Christian book-shops offering titles as diverse as 'Jesus, Son of God' and 'God, Father of Jesus'. Many people enjoy eating at this time of year, and they're well catered for in Portadown with its many shops selling food. Then . . . er, what else? Banks! Of course – there must be a dozen banks on the High Street, perfect for arranging that traditional Christmas overdraft.

(OK that's 100 words, fair enough – The Editor)

SAMARITANS

'At this special time of year, it is important not to think of those who are friendless and alone, as this will only depress you.'

This year's fight over the last loaf of bread in Sainsco's has been won by:

Mrs Rita McNally
54 The Development
Ballyhannon

Northern Ireland Electricity

'The men behind the wire'

What to do if you find yourself without power this Christmas:

■ Call 999

■ Take a deep breath

■ Say, 'OK, now I'm ready to join the Policing Board.'

A Christmas message from the Free Presbyterian Church

CHRISTMAS TREES ARE PAGAN IDOLATRY

'SANTA' IS AN ANAGRAM OF 'SATAN'

SHERRY TRIFLE COUNTS AS DRINK

The Portadown News would like to remind its readers of the true meaning of Christmas:
CONSUME OR DIE

New Year

New Year Honours

Bill Mason Snr MBE

For services to retiring without making a fuss

Barbara Menary OBE

For services to pets, charity, voting Alliance, that sort of thing

Sir Bob Stormont CBE DOE

For services to keeping quiet about water privatisation

Sir Gerald Adams OBE, MBE, CBE, IRA

For services to not killing anyone for another year

HOUSE-PARTY PANIC FOR LOCAL MAN

by our party correspondent, R. S. Veepee

Local man Brian Cunningham is sitting in his new £120,000 house right now, worrying that nobody will show up for his New Year's Eve party.

'My student parties were legendary,' Mr Cunningham told our reporter this morning, 'but I'm not sure people will want to spend the "best night of the year" stuck in a sterile development in the middle of nowhere.'

'Suppose just a handful of people turn up and then can't get a taxi home until 6 a.m.,' he added. 'God, I feel so alone.'

New year, new name?

by our North West correspondent, Dermont Londondermont

DUP councillors have tabled a motion to resolve Portadown's contentious town name issue once and for all.

'Many residents find the term "Port" highly offensive,' explained Councillor Marvin Currie yesterday.

'Port is an alcoholic beverage, and the God-fearing people of Ulster want no truck with the devil's buttermilk. Portadown must be renamed "Adown" immediately.'

The Portadown News

4TH JANUARY 2002 — www.PortadownNews.com

WHEN GERRY MET FIDEL

by our man in Havana, Green Graham

The Portadown News has obtained a top-secret CIA recording of Gerry Adams' meeting with Cuban President-for-Life Fidel Castro.

Today, we print an exclusive transcript of the two Great Leaders as they discussed the future of humanity.

Castro: "So Gerry, tell me what you have done to achieve World Socialism."

Adams: "We're now the third-largest party in devolved local government."

Castro: "What the *(inaudible)*! You murdered 2,000 people for that?"

Adams: "Now hang on a minute there, Fidel, Martin killed most of them. I just sent out the press releases."

Castro: "Well it's just not good enough, Gerry. We're supposed to have a Global Workers' Paradise by now."

Adams: "I've been telling the boys that for years, Fidel. But every time I say 'Worker', they just laugh at me."

Castro: "Maybe you should lose the beard. It makes you look like a geography teacher."

At this point, President Castro ended his audience with Mr Adams, and wished him "A safe journey back to England".

Pool ready for New Year crowds!

by our lifestyle correspondent, Ben Dover

80,000 litres of water have been drained from the Cascades swimming pool in Portadown, to make room for the traditional New Year influx of fat people.

"Every January it's the same," explained Cascades Manager Mr P.N. Poole yesterday. "Sickened by their appalling greed and disgusting obesity, hundreds of local people make a New Year's Resolution to go swimming every day."

"Fortunately," he added, "they all give up after about three weeks."

THINK OF THE CHILDREN

by our security correspondent, Roger Base

More trouble has broken out in North Belfast, after local residents were once again prevented from taking their children to a riot.

"It's terrible having the kids hanging around the house all day," local mother Millie Slapper told our reporter. "If things don't improve soon, I might even have to consider sending them to school."

Meanwhile North Belfast Sinn Fein MLA Gerry Kelly has appealed for calm.

"It is vital that law and order are restored," said Mr Kelly, *"As long as it's not by the forces of law and order."*

Northern Ireland declared WORLD HERITAGE SITE

by our historical correspondent, Hudda

The United Nations has declared Northern Ireland a World Heritage Site.

"This award recognises Northern Ireland's perfectly-preserved 16th-century political environment," UN heritage spokesperson Rusty Castle told a packed press conference yesterday. "Nowhere else in the world are so many mediaeval principles still standing."

It will now be illegal to change any part of the political landscape. "Fortunately," added Mr Castle, "there was fuck-all chance of that happening anyway."

STAY HEALTHY – START SMOKING

by our health correspondent, Florence Vulture

Health Minister Bairbre de Brun has urged people across Northern Ireland to take up smoking in the New Year.

"Smuggled and stolen cigarettes now represent Sinn Fein's main source of income," the Minister told a packed press conference yesterday. "If this business does not continue to grow, we may have to re-examine our political position – which could, of course, have serious public health implications."

Northern Ireland Forecast

BITTER

Northern Ireland Office

WARNING TO TERRORISTS IN NORTH BELFAST

Dear Brigade Commander

As part of our ongoing operations, we hereby place you on notice that you will not be shot. Also, you will not be arrested.

In fact, we really shouldn't be talking about this. Even though talking is the only way forward.

Hugs
Jane Kennedy
Insecurity Minister

Dodds condemns violence

by our politics correspondent, Jim Hacker

North Belfast DUP MP Nigel Dodds has issued a strongly-worded statement condemning the violence in his constituency.

"This is awful, terrible, really really bad," said Mr Dodds yesterday. "Dreadful, absolutely inexcusable, totally unacceptable."

"Still," added Mr Dodds, "it's all the fenians' fault you know. Vote DUP."

UDA PHONES IN SICK

by our paramilitary correspondent, P. O'Neill

There are renewed hopes of a breakthrough in North Belfast today after the UDA phoned in sick.

"We've got … the flu," an anonymous caller told Insecurity Minister Jane Kennedy this morning. "We can't make it in today. In fact, we might take tomorrow off as well. The codeword is Lemsip."

Ms Kennedy then asked the UDA if they planned to see the Doctor.

"Oh no, it's not that serious," said the caller. "We'll probably just phone Sammy Wilson."

Westminster graffiti scandal - *police baffled*

Local woman met Princess Margaret

by every newspaper in Northern Ireland

Local woman Violet Bluerinse has particular reason to be saddened at the recent death of Princess Margaret, for she met the Princess at a Buckingham Palace garden party 14 years ago.

"I'll never forget the wonderful conversation we had together," Mrs Bluerinse told our reporter yesterday.

"'So what do you do?' Her Royal Highness said to me as we stood in line beside the fox-burger stall." 'Well,' I said, understandably over-awed, 'I take mentally-retarded teenagers to the toilet at the Portadown Sexually Transmitted Diseases Clinic.'"

"'My goodness!', said the Princess to a small girl standing beside me.

'What lovely flowers!'"

Fireworks at Council meeting!

by our politics correspondent, Jim Hacker

There was chaos at Craigavon Borough Council's weekly meeting last Monday, when Loyalist protesters threw a lit firework at Sinn Fein Councillor Darren O'Hagan.

"I am absolutely appalled and amazed that Loyalists threw an explosive device, with a lit fuse, towards me," Councillor O'Hagan told our reporter yesterday. "Why are they still using fuses, when you can get a perfectly good timer from Maplins for £3.99? Fucking amateurs."

UVF TARGETS PAEDOPHILES

by our paramilitary correspondent, P. O'Neil

The UVF has announced a crackdown on paedophiles living in Loyalist areas.

"Touching kids up is much, much worse than blowing them up," explained UVF Business Development Manager Sam 'Shooter' Wilson (34) yesterday.

The UVF action has the full support of Mr Wilson's 16-year-old girlfriend, mother-of-two Shelly-Anne McFatt. "No young girl should have to give some 30-year-old bloke a blowjob," said Ms McFatt. "Not unless she really likes him."

The Portadown News

15TH FEBRUARY 2002

www.PortadownNews.com

Fancy a pint with the UVF?

Then why not visit

The UVF Bar

Thomas Street

The Management reserves the right to ask you to wash your Rangers top and shave your wife.

Fancy a pint with the IRA?

Then why not visit

The IRA Bar

Woodhouse Street

The Management reserves the right to ask you to park your car bomb a bit further away next time.

---

welcometocraigavonboroughcouncil
northernireland

NOTICE OF 6% RATE INCREASE FOR 2002

In accordance with local government regulations, we are hereby forced against our will to disclose how we spend your money.

Refuse Collection:	£15m
Administration:	£540m
Leisure Centres:	£20m
Plotting to close Leisure Centres:	£23m
Protection Money:	£80m
Kidding ourselves about tourism:	£850m
Printing unnecessary leaflets:	£35m
Torturing street vendors:	£80m
Paying people who haven't worked here in years:	£12m
Painting 'Disabled Parking Only' all over the place:	£27m
Processing bribes:	£84m
Responding to complaints:	£0.00.

Murder angers Adams

by our paramilitary correspondent, P. O'Neil

SINN FEIN president Gerry Adams has reacted angrily to the murder of Castlewellan father-of-one Matt Burns (26). Mr Burns suffered a Permanent Loss of Human Rights after being shot in the head by the IRA.

"I wish to say how very angry and upset I am," said Mr Adams, "that the SDLP were so quick to blame Republicans for this deeply regrettable internal matter. The SDLP is clearly in collusion with Special Branch – how else would they know right away that we did it?"

"By the way," added Mr Adams, "that guy was a drug dealer, you know."

Tourism scandal!

by our bribery correspondent, Bungdit Singh

THE NORTHERN IRELAND Tourist Board has been accused of fraud, deception, theft, dishonesty and misappropriation. "For many years, the NITB has lied to the public and wasted huge amounts of taxpayer's money," claims a damning report from the Public Accounts Committee. Among the accusations levelled at the Tourist Board are:

- Claiming that Northern Ireland has a tourist industry
- Claiming that tourism actually is an industry
- Counting students who come home to visit their parents as tourists
- Counting Germans who get lost on the border as tourists
- Pretending that the 12th of July is a 'folk festival'
- Pretending that murals are 'community art'

However it's not all bad news, as the report reveals that tourism supports several hundred well-paid jobs. Unfortunately, all these jobs are at the Northern Ireland Tourist Board.

Argos admits consumer scam

by our consumer affairs correspondent, Kaye Mart

Catalogue retailer Argos has admitted that its Portadown store's much-vaunted 'warehouse' doesn't actually exist.

"Yes, it's all a scam," admitted Manageress Belinda Frump at a packed press-conference yesterday.

"When we ring your order through the till, a text message is sent automatically to one of several Argos 'parashoppers' in the town centre. They buy your item from a normal shop, run around the back of The Mall, and set it on the magic Argos conveyor belt. I'd like to apologise to our customers for how incredibly stupid this must make them feel."

Initial suspicions about Argos were raised last week by local housewife Agnes McFatt. "I noticed that if I ordered something you'd normally buy in Wellworths, it arrived in 30 seconds," she told our reporter, "but if you order something you'd normally get in Shillington's, it takes three hours. That's when I finally cottoned on."

Trimble insult outrage!

by every newspaper columnist in Dublin

"DAVID TRIMBLE will have to learn that the new secular pluralist multicultural Ireland won't tolerate offensive outbursts from Protestants. It's true that Ireland may have been rather backward 800 years ago, but that's hardly the case today. Not only are there Romanian gypsies on every corner, but you can hardly walk down O'Connell Street without seeing a black man.

"PATHETIC"

"We've even had an Indian family move into our neighbourhood, and they've been made very welcome. No doubt they'll open a nice little restaurant somewhere and …" etc. etc.

SHOPPER DEFENDS DECISION

by our retail correspondent, Kaye Mart

Portadown pensioner Violet Bluerinse has defended her decision to use the express checkout in Tesco yesterday, despite having 18 items in her basket.

"I'm usually the first to complain about other people breaking the rules," she told our reporter. "However, I've never seen any connection between my own behaviour and this society's inexorable slide into anarchy."

STOP PRESS: Ulsterman arrested

by our abuse correspondent, Peder O'Phile

A LEADING ULSTER paedophile has been arrested in Chicago on charges of "perverting the English language". Stan Mallon, 62, was found to be in possession of several 'language aids', including a

European Union grant application form, and a copy of John Pepper's Ulster-English dictionary.

New cities announced

by our 'urban' correspondent, Fubu Gangsta

Lisburn and Newry have both been granted City Status, despite initial plans to award only one new charter in the province. "The granting of two awards recognises Northern Ireland's growth and dynamism," said Secretary of State Jock McThingy yesterday. "The fact that Lisburn is a Protestant town and Newry is a Catholic town has absolutely nothing to do with it."

Meanwhile, local Council Chief Executive Trevor Cloudy has expressed his disappointment at the failure of Craigavon's bid. "If we'd been successful, it would have looked great on my CV," he told our reporter yesterday. "Then I might finally have got out of this shithole."

Mr Rory O'Splitter, Crossmaglen
"The border must go! Except for the bit between my two petrol stations."

Mr Bertie Ahern, Dublin
"This is ridiculous. You can't just call a referendum for your own party-political reasons."

Mr Slartibartfast, Magarathea
"The border should stay. It has such lovely crinkly edges."

Republic says "No!"

by our abortion correspondent, Emma Brio

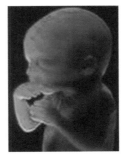

Following the no-vote in last week's referendum, the Irish government has announced new abortion guidelines for health professionals.

Termination will now be available to any Irish woman who has committed suicide. After receiving the last rites, the woman's body will be shipped to England where the foetus will be removed and posted back to her family in a jiffy bag. This should then be buried somewhere, and never mentioned again.

Pro-life campaigner Dana has criticised the new guidelines as "Secular liberalism gone mad".

QUEEN MOTHER DEAD – 54% of
Northern Ireland mourns

Slightly over half the population is this week mourning the loss of the Queen Mother, that much-loved symbol of Britain's grit, determination, class division and patronising attitude towards old people.

"She was the best of us, the heart of our nation, the century personified," Tony Blair told a hushed Commons yesterday. "Her death will certainly count amongst the darkest days of my presidency."

Ballymena Agricultural Show

SUNDAY WINNERS

PRIZE BULL

LAMB OF GOD

TOTAL COW

HORSE'S ARSE

Shock as train gets through Lurgan

by our Lurgan correspondent, Sam 'Spade' McNally

There were red faces on Lurgan's Kilwilkee estate last night as it emerged that a packed commuter train had been allowed to pass through the town without incident.

"It was amazing," an anonymous commuter told our reporter yesterday. "When we realised we'd actually got through Lurgan without being stoned or bombed, people started laughing and hugging each other," he said. "The atmosphere was brilliant. On days like that, I'm almost glad I can't afford a car."

Local Sinn Fein community representative Brendan 'Ninebar' McAlinden has now stepped in to assure Kilwilkee residents that the matter is being resolved. "The 5:35 from Belfast is always 20 minutes late through Lurgan," he explained. "However on the day in question, it was actually running on time, which caught local youth activists off guard. We believe this is an example of how British 'dirty tricks' are used to keep Republicans confused and demoralised."

"However," he added, "those responsible for yesterday's oversight have been kneecapped and their entire families exiled from Ireland forever, so I'm confident that train services through Lurgan will shortly return to normal."

HOAX CAUSES RAIL CHAOS

by our transport correspondent, Fred Petrolhead

There was travel chaos yesterday after dissident transport group the Rail NIR issued a series of hoax timetables. The no-warning publications contained fully-integrated bus and rail services with the potential, according to the RUC, to "seriously improve public transport throughout the Portadown area".

Now the NIR has hit back, describing the Rail NIR's aims as "completely unrealistic".

"Obviously we all want to see a fully-integrated public transport system," said the NIR in a statement released yesterday through Translink, its political wing. "However all of us on this island have to understand there are real differences between trains and buses, and any workable timetable will have to reflect that."

Cross-border chaos

by our security correspondent, Roger Base

The Real IRA caused further chaos this week with a series of hoax bombs on the telephone line at Lurgan. There were serious delays as cross-border phone calls had to be transferred between Moira and Portadown by post.

"A conversation that should have taken five minutes has ended up taking nine days," one disgruntled caller told our reporter this morning. "It took so long to get an answer back from Dublin, I'd forgotten my question. Is that the Real IRA's idea of a united Ireland?"

"On the other hand," she added, "maybe that *is* their idea of a united Ireland."

NEW CYCLE PATH ANNOUNCED

by our transport correspondent, Fred Petrolhead

The council has announced a new extension to Portadown's cycle path network.

"Cycling is the ideal form of transport for homosexual vegetarian communists," explained Council Chief Executive Trevor Cloudy yesterday. "It's important that these people have their own routes away from traffic, as many of them have obscene body piercings which can scratch your paintwork if you run over them."

The new Riverside Parkway Cycleroute will run from Buckfast Quay to a bog outside Derrytrasna, where the project will run out of money. It will then be abandoned for ten years, grow over with weeds, and be sold to a property developer.

Terrible train terror

by our security correspondent, Roger Base

There was more chaos for commuters today after dissident transport company the Rail NIR abandoned a suspect train on the line at Lurgan.

"The device contains several hundred tons of scrap metal in a highly unstable condition," confirmed PSNI Officer Bill Mason this morning. "It would be dangerous to move it."

A Translink spokesman has advised passengers to "buy a car, like a normal person".

The Portadown News

5TH APRIL 2002 www.PortadownNews.com

POLICE STATION STOLEN

by our security correspondent, Roger Base

Security chiefs are still baffled over the theft of Portadown Police Station. The redbrick Edwardian building disappeared late last night, leaving a large hole in the ground which has been sold to Tesco.

"A list of suspects has been drawn up," PSNI constable Bill Mason told our reporter this morning, "and asked to hold an enquiry."

Meanwhile, outgoing PSNI Chief Constable Ronnie Flanagan has reassured the public that the theft poses no threat to their safety. "I'd like to stress," said Sir Ronnie, "that Portadown Police Station contained nothing that could be of any use to anyone."

Gosford Castle sold

by our development correspondent, Des Res

A BUYER has finally been found for Gosford Castle, the largest private house in Ireland, which has lain largely unused since the Second World War. Businessman John Lawrence, who paid £5 for the sprawling Victorian folly, intends to develop it as a high-class brothel.

"Gosford's faux-medieval atmosphere will lend itself perfectly to bondage and fantasy nights," he told our reporter, "such as the ones I don't already run in Belfast."

An alternative bid to turn the castle into a Christian teaching centre was rejected by the planners as posing "a grave risk to local children". Local DUP Councillor Marvin Currie has welcomed the sale, but reminded the planning authorities of County Armagh's strict by-laws against anal fisting on the Lord's Day.

Budget 2002 - How will it affect you?

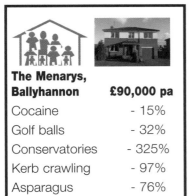

The Menarys, Ballyhannon £90,000 pa

Cocaine	- 15%
Golf balls	- 32%
Conservatories	- 325%
Kerb crawling	- 97%
Asparagus	- 76%
Verdict:	Laughing

The McNallys, Dirthole Street: £53.06/week

Buckfast	+ 15%
Scratchcards	+ 32%
Petrol bombs	+ 325%
Dogshit	+ 97%
Chips	+76%
Verdict:	Screwed

Confusing graphic

FEAR AS FEUD ESCALATES

by our security correspondent, Roger Base

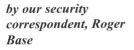

The streets of Portadown are tense tonight after a renewed escalation of the ongoing Cub Scout–Boy's Brigade feud. Trouble began yesterday morning, after several Cub Scouts confronted a group of Boy's Brigade members in a local sweetshop and called them 'a bunch of poofs'.

The Boy's Brigade later retaliated by telling local women that a leading Portadown Cub Scout has a badge in needlework.

"This feud most stop," one fed-up resident told our reporter yesterday. "They say it's political, but really it's just about who controls the pocket money."

Farmer's phone-mast victory

by our rural affairs correspondent, Grant Dole

Annaghmore farmer Josias Bogman is celebrating today after a successful campaign to prevent a mobile phone mast being erected on his property. "Mobile phone masts emit dangerous f-particle radiation," explained Mr Bogman to our reporter. "This causes salmonella, water pollution, mad cow disease, Range Rovers and all the other things blamed on farmers." "Fortunately," added Mr Bogman, "you can protect yourself against f-particle radiation with thick wads of cash, which I'm sure to get soon if I keep on making trouble. Now get off my land."

Lunacy Heights
Luxury living in a small concrete box

★ Electric kettle ★ Unbearable loneliness ★ Inflatable bedroom ★
Mahogany lightbulbs ★ uPVC toilet seat ★ Minutes from Sandy Row!

THIS WEEK'S SPEEDING EXCUSES

Craigavon Magistrate's Court has heard the following half-baked excuses for speeding on the M1:

– Mr Derek O'Hallion (95 mph)

"You can't prosecute me. I'm on ceasefire."

– Mr William Shankill (154 mph)

"My handler gave me permission."

– Constable Bill Mason (108 mph)

"I thought Special Branch were after me."

– Ms Nuala O'Loan (71 mph)

"If you give me penalty points, I'll kill myself."

ROADS Service

This week's Royal Motorway Closures

Tuesday
The M2 will be closed for six hours, while Princess Michael of Kent opens a mosque in Ballymena.

Wednesday
The M5 will be closed during morning rush-hour, while Prince Andrew flies over it in a helicopter.

Friday
The M3 will be closed all day, while the Dowager Duchess of Lanarkshire abseils down the BT tower.

Climate change fear

by our weather correspondent, Philip Angie

SCIENTISTS say Northern Ireland will experience increasing chaos over the next century, as the political climate doesn't change.

"We've been pumping huge amounts of crap into the air for over 400 years," explained Queen's University Climatologist Dr Bunsen McBurner yesterday. "But it hasn't made any difference."

However, Dr McBurner believes that Portadown and North Belfast will still hot up occasionally.

GOD TO TESTIFY AT SAVILLE INQUIRY

by our religious affairs correspondent, Helen Brimstone

Lord Saville has summoned God to appear before the Bloody Sunday Tribunal. Mr Jehovah God (15 billion), of no fixed abode, is believed to have been the Officer Commanding the Universe at the time of the shootings.

Among the questions Mr God is expected to face are: "Why do bad things happen to good people?" and "Why isn't life fair?" The Tribunal also wishes to know why Mr God is often referred to as 'The Lord', a title normally reserved for addressing Lord Saville.

Mr God's present whereabouts are unknown: he was last seen in the company of a young woman in the Bethlehem area, on the night of March 25th 1BC.

"If Mr God fails to attend the Tribunal, I will force him to appear," said Lord Saville, "possibly by finding the Ark of the Covenant and opening it, like in Indiana Jones."

Out with the West!

by our property correspondent, Des Res

West Belfast is to be renamed 'East Lisburn', after a long campaign by local estate agents. Thanks to its new address, a two-bedroom Executive semi in Ballymurphy will now cost £180,000.

West Belfast was partitioned from the rest of Northern Ireland in 1969, creating an artificial one-party 'state-let'.

Welcoming the move, East Lisburn MP Gerry Adams announced a new campaign to have Lisburn renamed 'North Hillsborough'.

Queen in border incursion row

by our royal correspondent, Benny Jond

The Irish Government has complained 'at the highest level' following an alleged border incursion by Her Majesty the Queen last week.

The sovereign breach of sovereignty occured on Tuesday morning, when a small force of Royals is understood to have crossed into Irish territory during a routine patrol of County Fermanagh.

However, Buckingham Palace has moved quickly to defuse the situation, with Prince Philip issuing a formal statement to the media.

"I suppose it is possible that we crossed the border without realising it," the Prince told reporters this morning, "as you bloody micks all look the same to me."

FANS RIOT AFTER MATCH

by our security correspondent, Roger Base

There was more trouble in North Portadown's Slimestone Road this weekend, after France beat Denmark in the World Tiddlywinks Final.

"The victory of Catholic France over Protestant Denmark represents another disgraceful concession to republicans," loyalist community representative William Shankhill told our reporter last night, while lighting a pipe bomb.

However, nationalist community leader Kerry Jelly has blamed the police for the trouble. "There weren't enough police officers on the ground," claimed Mr Jelly, "except for later on, when there were too many of them."

Notice of Election Results
East Central Dublin District

Brendan Bung (Soldiers of Bribery):	46%
Cahal O'Carbomb (Our Drugs Alone):	14%
Eamonn Useless (Fine Mess):	12%
Justin the Ostrich (Puppet Party):	15%
Nick O'Loan (Ind. Property Barons):	27%
Lord Dublin (Absentee Landlord):	n/a

Note: The Regressive Democrats were disqualified after failing the weigh-in.

Church vandalised

by our religious affairs correspondent, Helen Brimstone

Politicians from both sides of the religious divide have condemned last night's break-in at Portadown Free Baptist Church. Vandals poured Buckfast in the font, underlined sections of the Bible that contradict each other, and spray-painted 'Darwin Rules' over the organ.

"It's too early to speculate on a motive," Constable Bill Mason told reporters this morning, "but I'm afraid this bears all the hallmarks of a secular-humanist attack."

Belfast Culture Map

RIOT QUARTER

PUNISHMENT QUARTER

Cathedral Quarter

STUDENT QUARTER

ARSE COUNCIL of Northern Ireland

doktormoog@hotmail.com

ORGAN SCANDAL HORROR

by our medical correspondent, Florence Vulture

Health Minister Bairbre de Brun has strongly criticised Queen's University, after it admitted storing human organs without official permission.

"It's wholly unacceptable," Ms de Brun told reporters yesterday. "The correct way to deal with body parts is to bury them in a bog in County Louth, forget exactly where, then call anyone who complains about it 'an enemy of the Peace Process'."

PEACE PLAN AGREED

by our community correspondent, Grant Dole

STORMONT is considering a new North Portadown Action Plan, drawn up by community groups to help ease tension in the troubled neighbourhood. The recommendations include:

- Bullet-proof bus stops
- £20m indoor quad/bike stadium
- Sky Sports in DSS waiting area
- Weekly 'So Solid Crew' concerts
- Free chips for fat girls
- More reliable pipe bombs

"None of these things will make any difference," admitted one 'community spokesman' yesterday. "But we want them anyway."

Everything's just fine!

by the Northern Ireland Office

It's been another wonderful week of peace in Northern Ireland! Little Protestant and Catholic children skipped to school, where they enjoyed a comprehensive-style education which recognised all their unique abilities. Afterwards, they played together in the sunshine.

Meanwhile, their happily-married parents enjoyed another rewarding day at work in our many exciting new call centres, before travelling home on trains that didn't crash.

So really, there's absolutely nothing to worry about, and anyone who suggests otherwise is a very naughty policeman indeed!

© Jane Kennedy, Insecurity Minister

The Portadown News

10TH JUNE 2002   www.PortadownNews.com

2002 Rates Accounts

Trips to Columbia	£90m
Orchestrating riots	£15m
Paying protection money	£50m
Collecting protection money	£80m
Police non-liaison committee	£999
Kidding ourselves about tourism	£80m
Beard strimming	£35m
Torturing street vendors	£60m
Building world socialism	£12m
Building luxury homes in Donegal	£27m
Paying off the Alliance Party	£69m
Responding to complaints	£0.00

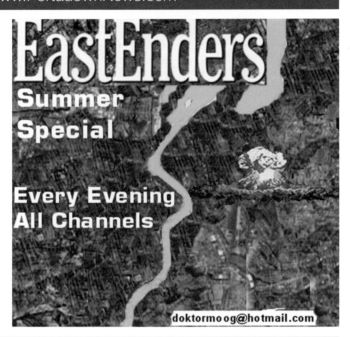

EastEnders
Summer Special
Every Evening
All Channels

doktormoog@hotmail.com

Castlereagh Police Station Canteen
Chef's Special

Security Leek Soup

Stuffed Pork (with Mange Tout)

Protective Custardy

Making Northern Ireland Safer

Burns Report Household Survey

I would like my children educated by:

A comprehensive system

A selection system   ■

A murderer   ■

*Please return your completed form
to the Department of Education,
c/o The Army Council*

Suicide enquiry call

by our health correspondent, Florence Vulture

The Northern Ireland Human Rights Commission has demanded a public enquiry into the deaths of Portadown terrorists Willy 'King Hamster' Bright and Martin 'King Gerbil' Sutton.

"The situation is totally unacceptable," said an NIHRC Spokesman yesterday. "Several hundred paramilitaries have been imprisoned since the signing of the Good Friday Agreement, yet the Government has so far only managed to kill two of them."

NEW COLLUSION PROBE LAUNCHED

by our collusion correspondent, Roz Bent

Northern Ireland's latest collusion probe will be launched tomorrow from Cape Canaveral, unless there's a mysterious fire in the control room.

The £1 billion 'Star Witness' probe will travel to the ends of the Earth and back. The probe is capable of detecting many different kinds of collusion, including infra-orange, ultra-violent and police-radio.

Asked where the probe should begin its investigations, a Special Branch spokesman said "Up Uranus".

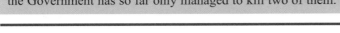

Why can't everything Orange be Fanta?

The Good Old Days

with Courtney Rosetint

This week's picture from Before The War shows Dirthole Street, which was finally demolished in the 1950s to make way for the space behind Jeffers. Amazing as it seems to us now, often as many as 40 people lived in a single one of these little terraced dwellings. To make room for everyone, the adults of the household would take turns to stand outside sobbing hopelessly, while the children slept hanging upside-down in cupboards.

None of the houses in Dirthole Street had a bathroom, as Before The War people rightly associated washing with homosexuality. Consequently everyone in Dirthole Street was very smelly, and sometimes the stench was so bad that shoppers in nearby Market Street would vomit into horse-troughs. Indeed to this very day, local people going into Portadown to fetch items for friends or neighbours will say, "I'll throw it up to you."

In 1928 Portadown Borough Council decided to act on the problem by decreeing that, "Henceforth all vomit collected in the town's horse-troughs shall be distributed amongst the poor and needy, preferably while still warm." The Welfare State had arrived!

---

with Courtney Rosetint

ALTHOUGH many troublemakers will tell it otherwise, it's important to remember that Before The Troubles, Portadown's Catholic community enjoyed the 12th of July just as much as their Loyal God-fearing neighbours.

This week's picture shows an Orange Parade crossing the town bridge in 1911. It was then customary for a delegation of Catholics to march down Obins Street at the same time carrying a large banner reading "No Hard Feelings". The two parades would meet at The Olde Sectarian

Interface near the present-day railway station, where the leader of the town's Catholics (or "priest") would present The Grand Master with a letter congratulating the Protestants on their victory at the Battle of the Boyne in 1690, and declaring that – as far as the Catholics were concerned – this marked "an end to the matter".

It is true that some trouble occurred back in 1875 when it was discovered that this letter had been written in Irish, but the matter was soon amicably resolved, with only a handful of casualties. Simpler times indeed!

The Good Old Days

www.PortadownNews.com

with Courtney Rosetint

This week's picture shows the Dirthole Street Annual Church Outing. Today the word 'outing' has sinister implications, its meaning perverted by the global homosexual conspiracy, along with other formerly decent words like 'gay', 'straight', and 'arse-fucking'. However, Before The War, an outing was a happy affair.

Obviously the outing could not take place on a Sunday, as Before The War everything was closed on Sundays and anyone seen outside while church bells were ringing was shot dead by the Black and Tans. So the children received a half-day from their factories on Saturday afternoon, for which they were docked a week's pay.

The happy day-trippers boarded the bus, boys on the left side, girls on the right. A large linen cloth impregnated with bromide was then hung between them to prevent acts of ungodliness.

After getting off the bus, usually in Dungannon, the children were marched to the edge of town and ordered to sit down in a field and eat sandwiches.

Religious music could be discussed, but not played. All too soon it was time to return to Portadown in time for nightshift. Simpler times!

with Courtney Rosetint

This week's picture from Before The War shows Christmas Day at the Dirthole Street Home for the Unwanted Bastards of Fallen Women.

Every year, the kindly warden Ebeneezer Gradgrind would send small Catholic children knocking on doors around Portadown begging for money. Indeed, this is the origin of the expression "Tiny Tim". Most returned alive, and the money they had collected was used to provide a traditional Christmas meal of roast swan for the Protestant children, who were (obviously) Less Fallen than the Tiny Tims.

"Mr Gradgrind was a saint who loved us all like a father," wrote one Unwanted Bastard in his 1975 suicide note. "He came into my room every Christmas morning dressed as Santa, and asked to see my sock. At least, I think that's what he said."

The Good Old Days

by Courtney Rosetint

This week's black and white picture shows residents of Dirthole Street celebrating the Queen Mother's visit to Portadown in 1962. Her Royal Highness passed directly over the town in a Vickers Viscount en-route to Canada, and personally ordered the pilot to descend 500 feet to be "nearer her beloved Ulster subjects".

Mrs Violet Bluerinse *(pictured centre)* still remembers hearing the Royal Aircraft's engines throttling back above heavy cloud. "It was the proudest moment of my life," she told me yesterday at Killicomaine Old People's Home. "We used to have a washing machine that sounded just like that. Or maybe it was the hoover."

Portadown held a week of celebrations following the Queen Mother's visit, after which the new Northway bridge was named 'The Flyover' in her honour.

with Courtney Rosetint

This week's old photograph shows Shorts during the war. The factory was busy then with orders for the F1916 long-term bomber.

"We had loads of work, cushy jobs and the highest wages in Belfast," remembers one former employee.

"Still even though the country was relying on us we went on strike at the slightest excuse."

Simpler times indeed!

Lookalikes

Nigel Dodds in 'Phantom of the Opera' shock

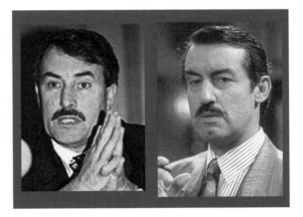

Mitchell McLaughlin in 'Boycie' from 'Only Fools and Horses' shock

Alliance Party leader David Ford in 'Ming the Merciless' shock

Martin McGuinness in Art Garfunkel shock

Loyalists attack students

by our education correspondent, Una O'Level

It's pipe bombs versus pipe bongs in South Belfast, as the Loyalist/Student feud reaches new levels of violence. "The main objection to students in our area is noisy late-night parties," explained UDA Brigadier Alan McGurk, "which we don't get invited to."

Meanwhile, student spokesman Cahal Chucky has strongly condemned the increasing number of attacks. "I really don't know why loyalists hate students so much," said Mr Chucky. He then repeated his comments in Irish, before calling our reporter 'a tool of the imperialist oppressor'.

FINUCANE CRISIS DEEPENS

Anybody know a good solicitor?

Mayor will attend Somme ceremony

by our Somme correspondent, Tommy Trenchfoot

Portadown's new Sinn Fein Mayor Alice Maskey has confirmed that she will be attending this year's Battle of the Somme Remembrance Service, at the town's new cross-community war memorial.

"At the Somme, thousands of Irish people – both Protestant and Catholic – were needlessly slaughtered," said the Lady Mayor yesterday, "and as a republican I have no problem with that concept whatsoever."

Dog on the Street The 'Community Representative Column'

An occasional feature where somebody you haven't voted for decides to speak on your behalf. This week: Loyalist Spokesman and TV Personality Billy Irvine.

"It's time Protestant and Catholic working class people realised that their real enemy is the bigoted middle class, which has tricked them into fighting each other instead of working together towards Building World Socialism.

"Of course when I use the term 'working class', I don't mean it in the old-fashioned sense of people who actually work. By 'working class' I mean community representatives who live in 'working class areas'. Ordinary people sometimes find this difficult to understand, but that's because they didn't do A-level politics in the Maze like what I done.

"I had that Leon Trotsky in the back of my cab the other day ...."

.... continued on all channels

CATHOLIC COUPLE HAVE PROTESTANT BABY

by our fertility correspondent, Urethra Franklin

A Catholic couple who had a Protestant baby are blaming the Sandy Row IVF Clinic for their horrifying fertility mix-up.

"We first noticed something was wrong after 18 months," the distraught mother told our reporter yesterday, "when we realised he was walking, but he wasn't talking."

The child has since barricaded himself into one corner of his bedroom, and is insisting that the people next door are his real parents.

FLOODS HIT ORMEAU

by our flooding correspondent, Denis Watermain

Residents have mounted a protest after last weekend's heavy rain led to wet feet on the Lower Ormeau Road.

"A large quantity of water came through our area without first seeking dialogue," explained Residents' Committee Staff Officer Paddy Rice yesterday. "As a result, we have asked the Flood Tribunal to monitor the situation."

"From now on", warned Mr Rice, "there'll be no precipitation without participation."

IRA Statement

Due entirely to 800 years of brutal British oppression, the IRA may have been indirectly involved in the killing of several people over the past 30 years.

As part of our courageous move towards peace, the IRA is now prepared to forgive some of those people. Later this year, after we join the Policing Board, we may consider forgiving the rest of them as well.

To demonstrate our sincerity, bereaved relatives may purchase a carton of 100 Regal King Size for the bargain price of £5, from all usual outlets. Please present a death certificate to the barman to obtain your discount.

Following this historic act of forgiveness, we expect there to be no further mention of the subject. Occasional Real IRA bomb attacks will occur to ensure your continued co-operation.

P. O'Neill
Republican Press Office
Stormont

PEER IN NEAR-MISS FEAR

by our historical correspondent, Courtney Rosetint

LORD BROOKEBOROUGH has escaped unhurt after a dastardly rebel attack upon his Fermanagh estate. His Lordship was attending Parliament when the Continuity IRA detonated an explosive device, causing minor damage to three maids and a butler.

"We shall continue our struggle until all Ireland is free of these absentee landlords!" said a rebel spokesman yesterday. He then picked up his harp and boarded a sailing ship for Boston.

Other dissident republican news:

- Dissident republicans blame Queen Victoria for potato famine
- Dissident republicans demand 'One Man, One Goat'
- Dissident republicans sell tobacco for 2 farthings per cart-load
- "We're not living in the past," say dissident republicans

Orangemember

Can Britain's Agents save the Executive?

starring

Dr Evil

and

Mini Me

Scary baby – yeah!

McGuinness denies membership

by our denial correspondent, D. Niall

IRA Army Council chief Martin McGuinness has denied ever being a member of the British government.

"I am not now, nor have I ever been, a member of the British government," said Mr McGuinness from his office in Stormont yesterday.

Despite the denial, security sources believe Mr McGuinness is 'inextricably linked' to the Department of Education, which has been responsible for some of the worst government atrocities of recent years.

Local court report

This week's list of minor punishments

The following worthless judgments were handed out this week at Westminster Magistrates Court:

Mr G. Adams (West Belfast) received three penalty points for trying to turn both ways at the same time. His solicitor asked the court to take a recent apology into account.

Mr D. Trimble (Portadown) received a caution for failing to drive in the middle of the road. His solicitor explained that Mr Trimble learned to drive on the extreme right, and occasionally forgets himself.

Mr M. Dog (North Belfast) received an unconditional discharge for a hit-and-run. Just like last time.

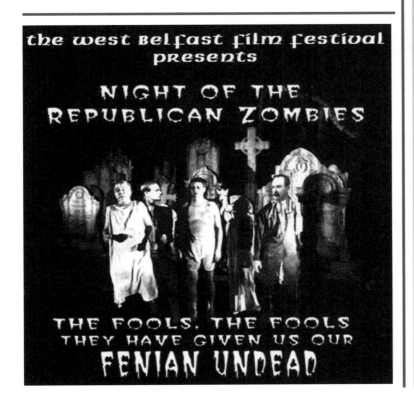

the west Belfast film festival presents

NIGHT OF THE REPUBLICAN ZOMBIES

THE FOOLS. THE FOOLS THEY HAVE GIVEN US OUR FENIAN UNDEAD

Policing breakthrough!

Hello? PSNI? I'd like to report an incident

The Portadown News

2002   www.PortadownNews.com

Thanks from Mayor

Portadown Mayor Alice Maskey has thanked the anonymous donor who sent her a bullet through the post this week.

It will be used to replace the bullet Martin McGuinness gave to General de Chastelain last October.

New Taxi Signs

TAXI (Orange)   Driver is a member of the UVF.

TAXI (Green)   Driver is a member of the IRA.

TAXI (White)   Driver knows where to get some coke, even at this time of night.

TAXI (Blue)   Driver is a registered sex offender.

LEGAL NOTES

The Northern Ireland Probation Board has issued the following guidelines for dealing with teenage rapists:

- **Victim's parents:** £2,000 fine for failing to offer a choice of contraception in a non-judgmental manner.
- **Victim:** A team of social workers will explain why it's all society's fault.
- **Rapist:** Six-month anger management course in Swiss Alps. Rehabilitation package to include snow-board hire and lift pass.

Fake results 'best ever'!

by our education correspondent, Una O'Level

Portadown Grammar School has announced its best-ever fake exam results. "Our 125% pass rate compares favourably with other fake exam results from around Northern Ireland," said headmaster Tim Godbarking yesterday.

This year's star pupil was Ruth Godbarking, who scored seven A* grades at A-Level. "I was particularly pleased with my results in astrophysics, neurosurgery and Ukrainian," explained Melissa, "as I didn't actually study those subjects."

Meanwhile, 5th-form pupil Nigel Molesworth has been burnt alive on the rugby pitch after receiving a B in GCSE Religious Studies. Speaking to reporters after the execution, his mother said, "I'm just glad that the shame is over."

'DAY OF PEACE' PLAN

by our politics correspondent, Reynard Hunter

Portadown's first anti-sectarianism rally will take place tomorrow. The event has been organised by the United Union of General Timeservers, who are promising 'several interesting speeches by Eamonn McCann'.

A large turnout is expected. Catholics should assemble in The Tunnel at 3 a.m. wearing Celtic tops, and proceed through the town centre singing 'The Fields of Athenry' in a boisterous manner. Protestants should assemble at Drumcree, wearing bowler hats, and proceed down the Garvaghy Road banging drums very loudly.

"We're confident that the rally will bring a day of peace to Portadown," said Union spokesman Jack Trotsky, "by keeping everybody as far away from each other as possible."

> Final score –
> Loyalists 1
> N. Ireland 0
> Well, there's a
> surprise ...

BACK FROM IBIZA!

The Portadown News meets some of the people currently annoying the whole town with stories about their summer holiday.

Tyler McSpide, 23
"Fuckin' class – them's what pills used to be like, like!"

Tania Slapper, 16
"... so I says to him, 'No! No! Oh, all right then'... "

Declan 'Decks' O'Hanlon, 32
"Of course, Cream hasn't been the same since Danny Rampling switched over to hard house blah blah blah."

Drumcree

Army demands better-looking women

by our security correspondent, Roger Base

The army has criticised civilian authorities for failing to provide soldiers with attractive women to look at during the Drumcree crisis.

"I've got 3,000 squaddies camping out in a field in July," explained Lieutenant-Colonel Julian Sandhurst, OC at the Mahon Fort, "and what have they got to keep their spirits up? Dara O'Hagan. It's completely unacceptable."

The Northern Ireland Office confirmed last night that it is considering shipping attractive women into the Portadown area for the duration of the crisis. "We're also investigating the theory," added the spokesman, "that Portadown's young men would spend less time throwing rocks at each other if they'd some chance of a decent shag."

Vatican sends Holy Water Cannon

by our security correspondent, Roger Base

Security sources have welcomed the arrival of a Holy Water Cannon from the Vatican City.

"Spraying Holy Water on Orangemen is pretty much like spraying ordinary water on them," admitted RUC officer Bill Mason yesterday. "But it will really annoy them, and that's the main thing."

Residents accuse media

by our media correspondent, Paige Green

Garvaghy Residents have accused the world's media of 'blatant triumphalism'.

"Who do these people think they are?" asked GRRC spokesperson Darren O'Hagan yesterday, "Coming into our neighbourhood in their 4x4s, prancing around in front of the cameras all fit and beautiful and smartly dressed."

"Say what you like about the Orangemen," added Mr O'Hagan, "at least they're as ugly as we are."

Orange Order awarded Victimhood Status

by our victimhood correspondent, Sue Mone

The Orange Order has been granted Official Victimhood Status at this year's Guardian Victimhood Awards in London.

"For many years the Orange Order spurned the idea of victimhood, associating it with moaning fenians going on and on about every tiny little thing like it was the end of the world," said awards presenter Jon Snow.

"However, the Orange Order's standing in society is now so low that we feel obliged to award it victimhood status anyway."

Mr Snow then presented Harold Gracey with a certificate confirming the Orange Order as "A Victim of its own Stupidity".

Killicomaine march passes off peacefully

by our Killicomaine correspondent, Barry Dogshit

The traditional republican July march through the loyalist Killicomaine housing estate passed off peacefully last night.

Residents came out to enjoy the spectacle as several hundred Catholics walked down Ulsterville Avenue banging bodhrans, waving tricolours and shouting, "Up the IRA, you Orange bastards!"

Local resident Tania McFattridge looks forward to the Republican parade every year. "Killicomaine was a Catholic neighbourhood before the Reformation, you know," she told our reporter yesterday, "so really we can't complain. It makes you wonder why they make such a fuss over Drumcree."

Apology

The Portadown News apologises unreservedly to Orange Order spokesman David Burrows for an article published last week in which we called him "A little Hitler". We completely accept that any resemblance between Mr Burrows and Hitler is purely physical, and deeply regret any offence this may have caused to the people of Germany.

Flanagan welcomes overtime

by our security correspondent, Roger Base

RUC Chief Constable Sir Ronnie Flanagan has described the Drumcree dispute as "a second Christmas" for his officers.

"As Orangemen like to point out, everyone in the RUC just loves the chance to make an extra few hundred pounds at this time of year," said Sir Ronnie yesterday.

"Obviously there's the small matter of risking your life, your family's life, possibly losing your home, suffering incredible stress, witnessing appalling violence and sinking into hopeless depression as the country you've sworn to serve spirals needlessly into anarchy. But if that's what it takes to pay off the sofa, then who really gives a fuck, eh?"

Perplexing Portrush power problem

by our business correspondent, Reg Empty

Portrush residents are celebrating tonight after planners refused permission for an offshore wind-farm.

Instead, the Assembly has asked American company CIA Energy to begin drilling for oil. A large oil rig will be anchored off the West Strand, with refining facilities constructed on the golf course.

"I'm absolutely delighted that my view won't be ruined by windmills," said some stupid woman who owns a shop on the sea-front. Her views were echoed by the DUP's Gregory Campbell, who believes that priests use windmills to hypnotise sheep.

Commenting on the pollution risk, a CIA Energy spokesman said, "We'll be locating the rig several miles out to sea, so very little of Portrush's litter should reach it."

This week's Loyalist death threats

Name: Neil Lennon
Crime: Playing for Northern Ireland without renouncing Rome
Verdict: Catholic

Name: Ian Paisley
Crime: Hasn't been seen at Drumcree for a while now
Verdict: Lundy

Name: Liz Windsor (Mrs)
Crime: Persistent refusal to have Duchess of Kent beheaded
Verdict: Traitor

Name: Basil Brush
Crime: Possibly named after the late Cardinal Basil Hume
Verdict: Judas

O'Splitter jumps bail!

by our crime correspondent, Rob Berry

A huge man-hunt is underway today after leading Portadown republican Rory O'Splitter jumped bail. Mr O'Splitter was released from prison last week to attend the launch of Gerry Adams' new book, 'Nobody Mention the War', available now for £1.99 from selected community centres.

"It is imperative that Mr O'Splitter returns himself to our custody," PSNI officer Bill Mason told reporters this morning, "so that he can be tried, sentenced, and immediately released again."

BBC RADIO BLUSTER

Seamus Austin talks to Sinn Fein's Mitchell McLaughlin
(followed by Sectarian Thought for the Day)

Seamus: "… so why won't you condemn attacks on Catholic police recruits?"

Mitchell: "Look! Look! The reality is that the police are attacking Catholics!"

Seamus: "So … attacking Catholics is wrong, but attacking Catholic police recruits is OK?"

Mitchell: "Absolutely, Seamus! Two wrongs make a right! Themmuns started it! Up the Provos!"

(continued until next election)

Equality for Ardoyne

by our equality correspondent, Billy Patrick Ahmed Cohen

As the new school year gets underway, Glenbryn Loyalists have applied to the Northern Ireland Equality Commission for permission to renew their protest outside Holy Cross.

"The Holy Cross protest is all about equality," Loyalist pastor Kenny McPipebomber told our reporter yesterday. "If we stop them fenians going to school, then they'll end up just as stupid as we are."

New policing row

by our security correspondent, Roger Base

Sinn Fein has criticised PSNI officer Bill Mason's offer to discuss loyalist death threats in person.

"Constable Mason doesn't understand," said a republican spokesman yesterday. "When we complain that the police aren't talking to us, that doesn't mean we want the police to talk to us. In fact, it means the exact opposite, unless Mitchell McLaughlin says it, in which case it doesn't mean anything."

"The police must co-operate with our refusal to co-operate with them," added the spokesman. "I hope that clarifies the matter."

Dear Claimant

Due to your politically inconvenient injury and/or bereavement in the Omagh incident, the Northern Ireland Office is hereby forced to award you the minimum £7,500 compensation as required by law.

As a result of your compulsory strip search, the following administrative charges will be deducted from your award:

- Rubber gloves   £5
- Vaseline   £ 3
- Torch batteries   £7
- Embarrassing the government with your private prosecution of the Real IRA   £7,485

Yours sincerely

**Jock McThingy
Secretary of State**

The Portadown News

Climate change fear

by our environment correspondent, Gaia Green

Addressing the Earth Summit in Johannesburg, First Minister David Trimble has warned the world's leaders that environmental problems pose a serious threat to Unionism.

"Rising sea levels will drive Britain and Northern Ireland further apart," predicted Mr Trimble, "while global warming will see many Southern animals migrating North."

After his speech, the First Minister answered a series of questions from the international media, such as 'Who are you?' and 'What's a Unionist?'

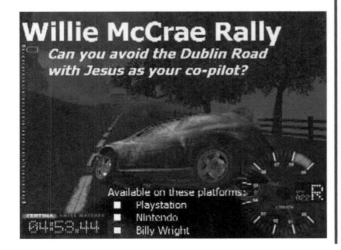
Dr Blunt's Photo Casebook

Trimble hasn't sold the Agreement

He's letting the hard-liners set the agenda

Jeffrey Donaldson makes me boke

And that David Burnside's even worse

I've got a headache

Me too

Dr Blunt writes: "The Ulster Unionist Party is a major cause of sexual dysfunction in the Portadown area. Try taking your mind off it with an addictive cocktail of anti-depressants."

RYANAIR HIJACK TAPES

PORTADOWN NEWS EXCLUSIVE!!!!!

Swedish police have released the cockpit voice recording of last week's Ryanair Stockholm–Stansted hijacking.

Hijacker: "This is a hijack! Fly to London."

Pilot: "We're already going to London."

Hijacker: "Stansted is nowhere near London."

Pilot: "But it has a convenient hourly train service to Liverpool Street!"

Hijacker: "Silence infidel! And don't think I'm paying for this cup of coffee either."

Meanwhile, security sources have denied earlier reports that the hijacker intended crashing the plane into central London. "No Ryanair plane has ever come within 50 miles of central London," said an MI5 spokesman this morning.

Portadown parties in the park!

by our clubbing correspondent, Charlie E. Grassman

Portadown partied late into the night this weekend, as superstar DJ Baldy Housemartin entertained thousands of revellers in the town park.

As well as dancing, concert-goers enjoyed many other exciting activities, such as drinking, taking drugs, fighting, falling over, and getting lost on the way to the chemical toilets.

'It was 12 non-stop hours of happy hardcore house techno,' said a man lying in a pool of his own vomit this morning, adding, 'I have no idea what that actually means.'

new series!
'I'M A CATHOLIC – GET ME OUT OF HERE!'

We've moved 50 Catholics into the middle of Larne. Who'll be the last one to get burnt out?

RIP Magazine

Gerry Adams shows 2,500 people around heaven

Also in this issue: Osama Bin Laden shows us around his lovely cave

Protect and Survive   **RADIATION HAZARD**

WHAT YOU SHOULD DO IN THE EVENT OF A SELLAFIELD MELTDOWN

1. Hold your breath
2. Walk in an orderly fashion to Donegal
3. Resume regular breathing
4. Use any hair that falls out to make an attractive Aran sweater
5. Wait for another statement from Jane Kennedy that everything is OK

Judith Lefty

Portadown's favourite columnist

'Terrible as they were, can the events of September 11th really justify war against Iraq? As an intellectual, I'm only interested in corruption, violence and human rights abuses when it's America's fault. Iraq is a 'third world country', so it can do what it likes, because poor people don't really know any better, do they?

Really it's no wonder people hate Americans, with their perfect teeth, highly amusing sitcoms and . . .'

continued for next two years

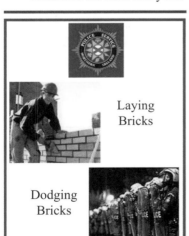

Laying Bricks

Dodging Bricks

IRA rejects monitor

by our ceasefire correspondent, B. Onduse

The IRA has responded angrily to David Trimble's request for an independent ceasefire monitor.

'This is pure Unionist mischief-making,' said an editorial in yesterday's Republican Business Post. 'The IRA ceasefire is intact. Anybody who suggests otherwise should report to their nearest Advice Centre for a knee-capping.'

BLOOMING MARVELLOUS

by our flower correspondent, Gerry Anium

Portadown has won first prize in this year's Blooming Towns award, picking up the top award in the 'Dreary Victorian market towns surrounded by supermarkets and industrial estates' category.

'Some people say Portadown is a bitter, dirty hole plagued by sectarianism and ignorance,' said Mayor Alice Maskey this morning. 'But just look at these lovely daffodils!'

STOP PRESS!
Corrs close Sellafield

British Nuclear Fuels has just announced that it is closing Sellafield as a direct result of last week's protest by Dundalk singing sensation, Jim Corr.

'Sellafield generates 15% of England's electricity,' explained BNFL Chairman Rod Spent this morning. 'However, that is insignificant compared to the energy behind The Corr's unique blend of 1970s soft rock with traditional Irish violin harmonies.'

UUP Council vote

UlsterUnionists

The following block votes were cast at yesterday's 4th Annual Ulster Unionist Party Unnecessary Crisis Meeting.

Against:

Donaldson's Own UDR Midgets	23
Ugly Women Waving Placards	14
Burnside's Kamikaze Ego Squadron	1
John Taylor's Chins	7
Betrayed Brethren	90
Jim Molyneaux's ex-girlfriends	0

For:

Everyone else	835

Hunting ban plan

by our hunting correspondent, Reynard Fox

The government is considering a ban on hunting Catholics.

Although considered cruel by most people, the traditional sport is still widely practised in many areas of Northern Ireland.

'We'll be protesting strongly against this proposal, which is an attack on our most valued traditions,' said a spokesman for the North Belfast Hunt this morning. 'Besides, if hunting is outlawed, what will we do with all our mad dogs?'

Disband the IRA? Don't be ridiculous

Loyalist Feud Exclusive!

by our loyalist correspondent, Billy Shootspatrick

The Portadown News can exclusively reveal that a dispute over drugs lies behind this week's outbreak of loyalist feuding.

'Moderate elements within the UDA prefer to skin up with a tobacco mix,' explained our source this morning, 'but hard-line elements won't settle for anything less than neat grass.'

Meanwhile, the LVF has heightened tensions by insisting that King Size papers are 'for poofs'.

The PSNI claims it is powerless to prevent the violence. 'Every time we go into loyalist areas,' said a police spokesman, 'we just get stoned.'

WEAPONS INSPECTOR APPOINTED

by our decommissioning correspondent, B. Onduse

THE UNITED NATIONS has appointed General John de Chastelain as its Iraqi Weapons Inspector. After arriving in Baghdad, the General will be blindfolded, strapped to a camel and led over the border to Saudi Arabia, where he will watch some concrete being poured into a hole in the ground.

Afterwards, Saddam Hussein will telephone Senator Ted Kennedy and promise to join the Secret Police Board, just as soon as the Republican Guard have all got jobs as bouncers.

'I'm confident that the Americans will be satisfied with this outcome,' General de Chastelain told our reporter yesterday. 'They were certainly happy enough with it last time.'

Music lovers!

Celebrate the marriage of Danny O'Donegal with this commemorative cake stand

Ideal for:

WEDDING CAKE

FRUIT CAKE

FAIRY CAKE

FUDGE FINGER CAKE

Only £69.69 inc. p&p
Please specify front or rear delivery

Anger in Columbia

Columbian community groups are demanding the expulsion of 'Bring Them Home' campaigner Catriona Ruane.

'Ms Ruane has shown great disrespect to our Latin culture,' explained 'Send Her Back' campaign co-ordinator Maria del Murte. 'Here in South America, we expect women to be friendly, attractive and clean-shaven at all times.'

Madam del Murte was formerly quarter-master of the West Bolivia Festival.

NERTEL REPAYS GRANTS

by our business correspondent, Reg Empty

Troubled telecommunications company Nertel Notworks is to repay £400,000,000 in government grants.

'We've scrounged huge sums of money off the taxpayer for construction, training and investment,' admitted a company spokesman yesterday, 'but now we'd like to give that money back, and let our shareholders bear the cost of management incompetence, like they're supposed to.'

Stop Press: The Portadown News has just learnt that this story is not true, and never will be.

'The Secret History of Gerry Adams'

by Ed Baloney, £19.16 from all good Advice Centres

Continuing our EXCLUSIVE serialisation of the book that's got everybody talking (to their solicitors) –

"As early as 1972, Sinn Fein's political project was beginning to take shape. 'Killing people is all very well,' McGuinness told Adams over tea and Jaffa Cakes at their Carryduff safe-house, 'but what really worries me is the injustice of the 11-plus.'

'Don't worry, love,' said Adams sweetly. 'Your day will come.'"

Next week – Danny Morrison fails his O-Levels

GOVERNMENT SUSPENDS REALITY

by our Agreement correspondent, Dale Sunning

In a last-ditch attempt to save the Good Friday Agreement, the Prime Minister has announced a temporary suspension of reality.

'Although reality has proved popular with the people of Northern Ireland,' Tony Blair told reporters yesterday, 'it hasn't worked too well at Stormont.' The alternative political arrangements being considered include:

- **Indirect rule**   Northern Ireland will be ruled from London, via Bristol
- **Joint Authority**   A cross-border committee will get very stoned, then order a pizza
- **Welsh Devolution**   Like ordinary devolution, except nobody cares

New fears for feud

by our Loyalist correspondent, Billy Shootspatrick

The main Protestant churches have announced an initiative to prolong the Loyalist feud.

'There is widespread concern throughout the community that the Loyalist feud will end before they've all killed themselves,' said Pastor Kenny McFlintlock yesterday. 'To address these concerns, we'll be meeting with each of the Loyalist groups, and telling them that the others are selling cheaper drugs.'

BBC Northern Ireland

'Sky High'

Christine Bleakley goes to Craigavon, where she meets a drug dealer, a heroin addict, and a kid who's sniffed so much glue that his tongue is stuck to his teeth.

The Portadown News

14TH OCTOBER 2002   www.PortadownNews.com

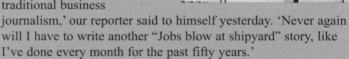

The Postman Always Photocopies Twice

POLICE ADMIT MISTAKE

by our security correspondent, Roger Base

PSNI Chief Constable Hugh-Hugh Barleymagrew has admitted that last Friday's raid on Sinn Fein's Stormont office was a mistake.

'We were looking for intelligence,' he told reporters yesterday, 'but all we found was Gerry Kelly.'

Republican Pony Trekking

Ride two horses at once!

£19.16/hour
(includes blinkers)

IT'S THE END OF AN ERA

by our business correspondent, Reg Empty

This week's final round of redundancies at Harland & Wolff marks the end of an era in Northern Ireland.

'This sounds the death-knell for traditional business journalism,' our reporter said to himself yesterday. 'Never again will I have to write another "Jobs blow at shipyard" story, like I've done every month for the past fifty years.'

> How DARE the British Government tell Unionists what to do!

Chaos in Colombia

by our Colombia 3 correspondent, Charlie Mortar

There was more chaos in Bogotá yesterday after the Colombia 3 once again refused to appear in court.

'My clients have no chance of a fair trial,' a lawyer for the accused told waiting reporters. 'Their case has been prejudiced by the fact that they are obviously guilty.'

TOURIST BOARD 'WASTE OF SPACE'

by our fraud correspondent, Grant Dole

GOVERNMENT watchdogs have strongly criticised the Northern Ireland Tourist Board for constructing a giant orbiting space mirror 150 miles above Hillsborough.

The £185 billion project aims to boost tourism by increasing the amount of sunshine in resorts such as Lurgan and Glengormley.

'Bad weather is not why tourists avoid Northern Ireland,' complained Public Accounts Committee chairman Sir Angus Charterbean yesterday. 'They avoid Northern Ireland because it's a nasty, dirty little hole.'

'The space mirror has been a horrendous waste of money,' added Sir Angus. 'It reflects very badly on the entire province.'

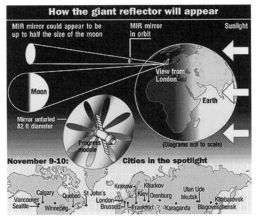

Direct-rule Ministers

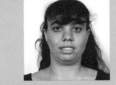

TOBY GUARDIAN (ISLINGTON NORTH)
Minister for Fraud, Bribery and Tourism
An enthusiastic socialist during his years at Eton, Mr Guardian aims to spend his time in Stormont 'keeping an eye on that bastard John Reid'.

LIZ BLAIRBABE (SOUTH STAINS)
Minister for Fluffy Kittens
Selected by her local party for having no opinions of her own whatsoever, Ms Blairbabe lists her interests in Who's Who as 'Doing whatever Tony says'.

SHOCK POLL RESULTS!

An exclusive poll commissioned by the Portadown News shows that support for the Agreement has fallen dramatically amongst people who never supported it in the first place.

Q: If the Good Friday Agreement referendum was held again tomorrow, would you vote for it?

Catholics: 100%
Protestants: 0%

Q: If you'd ever bothered reading the Agreement, and understood what it meant, would you vote for it?

Catholics: 0%
Protestants: 100%

Dilemma for local boy

by our crime correspondent, Rob Berry

PORTADOWN youngster Keanu Wilson (aged 9) faced a tough decision last night: whether to rob a bus-driver to pay for some sweets, or rob a sweet-shop to pay his bus fare. In the end, he hijacked a bus, drove it into a sweet-shop and went home in a stolen car.

'It's difficult being a kid these days,' Keanu told our reporter this morning. 'You've just got so many choices.'

Larne loyalist threat

Having burnt out the entire Catholic population, loyalists in Larne have issued threats against a series of other targets.

These include: Greengrocers, Republican-publicans, Irish setters, Cross-border collies, Gerryatrics and Virgins.

'All right-thinking people will condemn these threats,' said DUP Councillor Marvin Currie yesterday. 'But only very quietly, from behind the sofa.'

Shock over arms haul

by our loyalist correspondent, Billy Shootspatrick

Police sources have expressed their surprise at the discovery of a significant loyalist arms cache at the home of a loyalist on the loyalist Rathcoole estate.

'It is unusual for us to find such a large number of loyalist weapons,' said PSNI Officer Bill Mason yesterday, 'because we rarely bother looking for them.'

SEAL VIRUS – FARMERS CONCERNED

by our agriculture correspondent, Culchie McMucker

The Northern Ireland Farmer's Union has expressed 'deep concern' about the mystery virus killing Northern Ireland's seals.

'Animals are dying in large numbers,' said NIFU Chairman Josias Bogman yesterday, 'yet our members haven't received one penny in compensation.'

Mr Bogman admitted that his members don't own any seals, but pointed out that local farmers regularly receive compensation for cows, pigs and sheep that they don't own.

'In fact we should receive extra compensation for this disease,' added Mr Bogman, 'as on this occasion we probably didn't cause it.'

UNITED IRELAND CLOSER

by our united Ireland correspondent, Tony Wolfe

The Continuity IRA say this week's bomb alerts across Belfast have increased the likelihood of a united Ireland.

'Some republicans believe the road to a united Ireland lies through compromise and dialogue,' explained a Continuity IRA spokesman yesterday. 'But we believe it involves being stuck in traffic for five hours while a sniffer dog checks out a Citybus. Tiocfaidh ár lá!'

OMAGH – EVERYONE KNEW

by our security correspondent, Roger Base

The Portadown News has learnt that the entire population of Ireland knew about the Omagh bomb in advance, except Sinn Fein's Laughlin McMitchell.

'I still have absolutely no idea who planted the bomb,' Mr McMitchell told our reporter yesterday, 'and anyone who does know should under no circumstances tell the SS-RUC-PSNI-GAA anything, even though they already know all about it. I hope that makes Sinn Fein's position clear.'

National Front back

by our fascist correspondent, Wilhelm Shootspatrick

The National Front is to stand candidates in Northern Ireland elections. The party believes its anti-immigration policies will be a great success across the province, as asylum-seekers don't want to come here anyway.

Republicans have reacted angrily to the news. 'I can't believe these fascists are coming over here and taking our jobs,' said a Sinn Fein spokesman yesterday. 'They should go back to their own country.'

Jobs blow for South Belfast

by our business correspondent, Reg Empty

South Belfast's largest employer, 'Imagine Belfast', has collapsed with losses of £1.5 million.

'Staff face a bleak future,' said local MLA Hannah Camel yesterday. 'Most of them have only ever worked in this traditional industry, and have no other useful skills.'

'I'm not sure what I'm going to do,' admitted one former Imagine Belfast employee this morning, while sitting on a plastic chair at the Botanic Avenue JobClub, 'but my uncle works for the Arts Council, so whatever I end up doing, it should pay at least £80,000 a year.'

THE UDA. DON'T CROSS US, OR WE'LL CROSS YOU.

'Straight Quarter' plan

by our alternative lifestyles correspondent, Ben Dover

Plans have been announced to build a 'straight quarter' in Portadown. The development will include bars, restaurants and nightclubs where men and women can meet someone decent for a change.

'It's total unnatural,' an angry Pastor Kenny McFlintlock told our reporter yesterday. 'If God meant Portadown people to find attractive sexual partners, he wouldn't have put us between Lurgan and Dungannon.'

Portadown Borough Council
New Household recycling regulations

Please sort out your rubbish into the two separate bins we have forced you to buy for £60 each. These will be collected by our Accredited Waste Management Contractor and dumped into the nearest river.

BLUE BINS	YELLOW BINS
Buckfast bottles	Baby poo
Unopened junk mail	BSE-infected cattle
Spent cartridges	Gospel leaflets
Used pornography	Sump oil
Vegetables	Kittens

FUEL FRAUD CRACKDOWN

by our business correspondent, Reg Empty

Police have closed down another illegal fuel operation. Officers raided an address at 11 Downing Street, London, seizing several dishonest policies and a 3-litre Jaguar converted to run on Chardonnay.

'This outfit was costing the taxpayer billions,' said PSNI officer Bill Mason yesterday. 'Illegal taxation destroys small businesses and is a menace to society.'

A Scotsman is helping police with their inquiries.

Immigrant workers scandal

by our agricultural correspondent, Culchie McMucker

Eastern European immigrant workers on Ulster's farms are to receive official recognition in a bid to improve their working conditions.

'By reclassifying our slaves as "cattle", we'll receive grants to feed and house them,' explained Northern Ireland Farmers Union spokesman Josias Bogman yesterday, while parking his Range Rover outside his 8-bedroom house in South Armagh.

'We'll also receive proper compensation if they die, instead of having to dump their bodies in a ditch somewhere and letting the council sort it out.'

'Farmers want to treat our slaves with dignity,' added Mr Bogman, 'as long as it doesn't cost us a penny.'

welcome to Derry*

*Health Warning: Visits may be subject to Sinn Fein approval

Thumbs up on Monday!

Fingers up on Tuesday!

NORTHERN IRELAND FIRE BRIGADE
'Get out, all out, stay out'

Sinn Fein
SPY HARD

The Portadown News

18TH NOVEMBER 2002   www.PortadownNews.com

'THINK OF THE CHILDREN'

by our children's correspondent, Peder O'Phile

The annual 'Children in Need of Some Discipline' appeal takes place tonight, with people across Portadown coming together to give the town's little bastards a lesson they'll never forget.

The first event takes place in Sainsco's car park at 6 p.m., where a team of social workers will demonstrate how to give a good clip round the ear. PSNI officer Bill Mason will then illustrate the dangers of throwing stones at cars, by shooting kids off the Northway footbridge with a rifle.

POLICE SERVICE of NORTHERN IRELAND
A Service to be Proud of

Every other police force in the country believes staggered opening hours reduce violent crime.

However, it's a lot of paperwork and we really can't be arsed, so why don't you all just

GO HOME NOW!

Och Aye Way Hae, etc.

by our Ulster-Scots correspondent, Peder O'Phile

THE ULSTER-SCOTS BOORD has welcomed a police statement that loyalist criminal gangs are operating in Scotland.

'This exciting development highlights the strong cultural links across the North Channel,' said Boord Big Yin Lord Haggis yesterday.

'Also, unlike everything else we've received £4.1m of tax-payer's money to promote, the loyalist connection between Northern Ireland and Scotland actually exists.'

NEW! COMMUNITY BEAT

With Community Constable Barbara Brownshirt

'After last weekend's totally unacceptable attack in Andersonstown, I appeal to anyone with information about those involved to pass it on immediately to "the usual organisations", and certainly not to the police, otherwise you might end up meeting three men in a dark alley yourself.'

NEXT WEEK:
Constable Kelly offers you 10 pills for £30.

First Minister insult outrage!

by our Republic of Ireland correspondent, Una O'Culture

There is widespread anger in the Irish Republic after David Trimble referred to the popular European country as 'a complete sh*tehole'.

'. . . and Bertie's is only this big.'

'It's a tip,' the First Minister told reporters from the Chicago Fenian yesterday. 'They have these funny little statues at all the roundabouts, the mobile phone coverage is awful, and you can't drive anywhere without getting stuck behind four nuns in a Metro.'

The Irish government has angrily rejected Mr Trimble's remarks. 'Sure, you rarely see anyone driving a Metro these days,' said a Dublin spokesman this morning. 'I'd also like to point out that no politician down here has ever said anything rude about Northern Ireland.'

Other countries Mr Trimble doesn't like:
France – 'Surprisingly Catholic'
Australia – 'Too Southern'
England – 'Everybody laughs at me'

NEW NAME AGREED

by our 'North West' correspondent, Dermont Londondermont

Derry City Council has agreed a new non-controversial name for the historic city, ending years of embarrassment for inhabitants and newsreaders. Northern Ireland's second city will now be known as the Foyle Urban Conurbation, or FUC for short.

'This is a great day for both FUCing communities,' one FUCer told our reporter this morning. 'I think everyone can agree that the new name describes this city perfectly.'

Birmingham Four to discuss New Lodge Six with Colombia Three

by the Portadown News One

FULL STORY PAGE 2

Dolly Parton Attends All-Party Talks

Are those pair for real?

Tonight on SKY 4

8:00 Police! Tornado! Surgery!
Striking prison officers chase a tornado through the Royal Victoria Hospital Children's Ward, while Frank Mitchell warns you not to attempt organ transplants at home.

9:00 Celebrity Vets in Homicide
A star-studded cast of veterinary pathologists pursue a brutal serial killer by examining the entrails of a dead dog.

10:00 Celebrity Shipwreck Autopsy Challenge
Les Dennis dissects the rotting corpse of Myra Hindley on the deck of a sinking supertanker, as Anne Diamond entertains a live studio audience with heart-warming stories about her dead baby.

To evict Les Dennis call 0898-4321
To evict the tornado call 0898-4321

Cold turkey for Nesbitt

by our retail correspondent, Kaye Mart

James Nesbitt has been dropped from Belfast's Christmas advertising campaign after revelations of drug-taking. Mr Nesbitt was unavailable for comment today as his phone has been disconnected.

'Under no circumstances can the use of drugs be associated with shopping in Belfast,' a Council spokesman told reporters this morning, 'except possibly in North Street.'

The campaign will now be fronted by Gerry Kelly.

Toys I'R'A

Hundreds of toys direct from Florida!

Note to parents: Some toys may contain guns and live ammunition. Not to be used without permission from Uncle Gerry.

NEW WATER CHARGES *Water* Service

Glass of water	5p
Toilet flush (no. 1)	10p
Toilet flush (No. 2)	25p
Shower	£1.00
Shower (with friend)	£1.50
Filling Water Service Chief Executive's swimming pool	FREE

Miss Lurgan flees to Nigeria

by our Lurgan correspondent, Sam 'Spade' McGrath

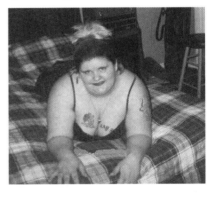

Miss Lurgan finalist Shelley-Ann McAvoy has arrived safely in the Nigerian capital of Lagos after her home town was torn apart by riots earlier this week.

Trouble flared in the notorious County Armagh trouble-spot after local republicans were denied their human right to rob a bank by fascist SS-PSNI storm-troopers.

'I'm just glad to get out of that hole,' said Miss McAvoy (17), who lists her interests as world peace, Buckfast and having children with animals. Asked if she was concerned about ethnic tensions in Nigeria, Ms McAvoy replied, 'I thought everyone here was black.'

Loyalists to help hospice

by our loyalist correspondent, Billy Shootspatrick

Loyalist mediation service the Ulster Paramilitary Research Group has offered to help in the Portadown Hospice crisis.

'Feuding over money while innocent people die all around you is right up our street,' explained a UPRG spokesman this morning. 'Plus we've got a huge stash of "painkillers" they might be interested in.'

NEW NAME FOR SHINNERS

by our paramilitary correspondent, P. O'Neill

Derry City Council has voted to re-name Sinn Fein. The popular baseball bats-to-pharmaceuticals corporation will now be known as 'The IRA'.

'This will avoid confusion when marketing the organisation to overseas investors,' explained IRA councillor Laughlin McMitchell yesterday. 'Besides, everyone's called Sinn Fein 'The IRA' for years now anyway.'

VANISHING VOTERS MYSTERY

by our electoral fraud correspondent, Ken Tuckyfriedchicken

GARDAI in County Louth are searching for bodies after reports that 20,000 people have disappeared from West Belfast.

'They were last seen at the 2001 assembly elections,' Garda Liam O'Mason told reporters yesterday, 'usually twice.'

Republicans have denied responsibility. 'We did not make these people disappear,' said a Sinn Fein spokesman this morning. 'Quite the opposite, in fact.'

Colombia Three re-trial

by our Colombian correspondent, Charlie Mortar

Following complaints from Danny Morrison, authorities in Bogotá have arranged a new trial for the Colombia Three.

'The suspects will be taken to a house in the West of the city and beaten for several days until they "confess",' Colombian Justice Minister Gerry Garcia told reporters yesterday. 'The judge will then be arrested while jumping out of the bathroom window, go to jail for a few years, and spend the rest of his life writing some of the worst short-story collections ever released by a serious publisher.'

A Sinn Fein spokesman has described the new arrangements as 'entirely fair and reasonable'.

The Portadown News

16TH DECEMBER 2002   www.PortadownNews.com

On the move

People going places in Portadown's ~~Golf Club~~ Business Community

Donald McSaunders has been hired as an Illegal Immigrant Intimidator by the May Pork meat-watering factory, to stop people taking a day off at Christmas.

Kieran Tapping has been appointed Chief Rates Adjustor for the Portadown area. He will assess people for the new Water Tax depending on how badly they smell.

Terrorists 'have smallcox'

by our paramilitary correspondent, P. O'Neill

A lovely big gun yesterday

Northern Ireland's terrorists have smallcox, according to a shock intelligence report leaked to the Portadown News this week.

The feared disease, which mainly afflicts young men, is infectious up to a distance of four inches. Symptoms include a rash outbreak of bile, followed by brain failure. There is no cure, although many sufferers find that owning a lovely big gun makes them feel more comfortable.

Miss Shelley-Anne McAvoy (17) was the victim of an UVF smallcox attack last year. 'It was extremely embarrassing,' she told our reporter yesterday, 'although to be perfectly honest I hardly felt a thing.'

6:00 Old Firm Rioting

Two teams of bigoted morons hurl bricks at each other in a futile attempt to give their lives some meaning.

7:00 Regional News

Two teams of 'community representatives' blame the police and each other for today's Old Firm Rioting, so condemning their communities to another cycle of wanton destruction.

8:00 Julian's in Your Tube

But not to worry! Here's a sad old ponce to cheer you up with a tragic camp routine that harks back to the sexual insecurities of a more innocent time.

LETTER TO THE EDITOR

Dear Sir

I am trying to trace my family history and would appreciate any information your readers can give me. My Great Great Grandfather Seamus O'Sheen was forced to leave Portadown in 1492 after a leprechaun stole his potatoes. He sailed to America on the Titanic, where he was rescued by Great Great Grandmother from an evil English actor. After settling in Boston he changed his name to 'Cheeseburger' so that he could buy some black people to scrub his feet.

Yours sincerely

Brad Cheeseburger, Boston

BRIGHT FUTURE FOR DIY SUPERSTORE

by our retail correspondent, Kaye Mart

Niall Wood, Manager of Craigavon's giant new B&Q Superstore, is looking forward to a bright future.

"Almost an entire generation of Northern Ireland people have committed their whole life's earnings to buying a nasty little house in a development somewhere," he explained yesterday.

"They'll never have the money to go out at night or away at the weekend, so they've no choice but to spend what little disposable income they still have on tacky DIY projects, vainly hoping this will bring some fleeting moment of happiness to their sterile, futile, materialistic existence.

"Here at B&Q we welcome customers with a friendly smile," added Mr Wood. "Yet – in our hearts – we weep for them."

Thought for the Day

Heavens Above!

with evangelical pastor Jeremiah Jones

Often, living in Northern Ireland, we face situations in our dealings with the world where our Christianity is sorely tested. At times like these, a Good Christian should ask *"What would Jesus do?"*

The answer, of course, is that Jesus would keep his head down, move to a nice development somewhere, wash the car once a week, have sex with the lights off, and pretend that everything else going on in the country is somebody else's problem.

Next week: *What would Satan, Dark Lord of the Underworld, do?*

Ulster-Scots Wae Hae!

Teach yourself the language of the Glens:
THIS WEEK'S WORD:
Paedophile - Wee'un Worrier

Tesco Traffic Lights,
Meadow Lane

"The world's slowest traffic lights"

FEBRUARY TIMETABLE

Monday
Green

Tuesday
Amber

Wednesday
Red

Thursday
Green

Friday
Amber

Saturday
Red

Sunday
CLOSED

Interesting talk at W.I.

by our women's features editor, Gayle Tinkerbell

Portadown Women's Institute will be hosting a talk tomorrow evening by local Committee Member Barbara Menary, entitled: "Multiple Orgasms: A Marxist-Leninist Perspective".

Afterwards, Mrs Menary will drink a bottle of sherry, then tell everyone that she thinks she's a lesbian.

Christmas

Cheers as some girl from TV turns on Xmas lights

by our Christmas lights correspondent, Osram Watt

PORTADOWN'S Christmas lights were officially switched on last night by local 'Popstars' finalist Gemma Frump (aged 15). Gemma shot to fame earlier this year when a live TV audience of 12 million watched her slashing her wrists after being described as 'too fat' by a star-studded panel of celebrity judges.

'Appearing on "Popstars" gave me just enough fleeting fame to make the rest of my life seem pointless,' Gemma told a cheering crowd of shoppers. 'As I switch on these lights, consider the darkness consuming my soul.'

New Year

New Year Come-down?

Then you need to take

ALCOHOL

Dose: 4 pints every 2 hours

Warning: Relieves symptoms only – your head is still fried

Portadown Panto 2003!

Growing frustration at assembly closure

by our education correspondent, Una O'Level

Portadown High School's assembly hall remains closed as pest-control experts search for moles. Although the building looks undamaged, school authorities say the moles may have eaten away at vital structural supports.

Students are growing impatient at the delay. 'We spent most of our time in assembly mucking about and listening to boring announcements,' one told our reporter yesterday, 'but it was still better than having to learn stuff.'

Auditions continue for Portadown boy band

by our music correspondent, Danny O'Flute

Portadown music promoter Pete Bogman is to hold another round of auditions for the town's first-ever boy band. The initial round of auditions, held in the town hall before Christmas, attracted hundreds of hopefuls, but only three of the proposed group's four places have so far been filled.

"Any successful boy band needs four distinct members," explained Mr Bogman yesterday. "A good-looking one, a gay one, a fat one and a stupid one."

"Unfortunately," continued Mr Bogman, "we only seem to be able to fill three of these categories locally."

Mr Bogman refused to say which one of the four categories remains open. "Let's just put it this way," he told our reporter. "We don't need to see anyone else from Portadown Grammar."

The Portadown News (Editor – N. Emerson) is printed at your expense by W. G. Bribe Ltd (Proprietor – N. Emerson)

The Portadown News

6TH JANUARY 2003   www.PortadownNews.com

MISSING
Orange Panda
(Bigotus Ignoramus)

Members of the public are advised not to approach the Orange Panda, as it is extremely aggressive and stupid when cornered.

ABORTION FERRIES

'Exporting Ulster's sexual hypocrisy to England since 1922'

Return cabin £50

Please do not steal the coat-hanger

ULSTER 'DOOMSDAY PLAN' SHOCK

by our security correspondent, Roger Base

The government considered re-partitioning Northern Ireland during the worst years of the troubles. Under the 1972 plans all women would have been moved to the West of the province and all men to the East. It was hoped this would ease sectarian tensions by gradually reducing the population to zero.

Although Prime Minister Ted Heath liked the idea of an all-male region, the plan was shelved after officials in Lurgan were unable to tell men and women apart.

The 1972 cabinet papers also reveal that IRA gunmen in West Belfast were paid £300 by the British Army to stop shooting people. Today, buying off a murderer costs £120,000 a year plus car plus benefits.

Ulsterman's polar triumph

by our polar correspondent, Ann Tarctic

The first Ulsterman to reach the South Pole has expressed his joy at being as far away from Northern Ireland as it is possible to be without actually leaving the planet.

'It's brilliant down here,' Barry Cummings told our reporter via carrier-penguin yesterday. 'In fact the only problem with being at the South Pole is that it's North in every direction.'

US ATTACKS NORTH KERRY

9TH MARCH 2001

by our American correspondent, **Brad Cheeseburger**

Hundreds of inbred farmers are feared dead today after America accidentally attacked North Kerry.

Pentagon officials are blaming voice recognition software on their latest 'smart' cruise missiles.

'I'm absolutely certain we said "North Korea",' explained a Pentagon official yesterday. 'Anyway, North Kerry voted Sinn Fein and they won't co-operate with weapons inspectors either, so it's all much the same at the end of the day.'

Church child abuse crisis

by our child abuse correspondent, Peder O'Phile

Ireland is in shock this weekend after the Catholic church admitted abusing generations of children placed in its care.

The Portadown News understands that thousands of priests and nuns conspired to damage impressionable young people by telling them a load of nonsense about virgins, saviours, angels and miracles.

'We have all been traumatised by our ordeal,' explained one victim yesterday. 'Still, at least the Protestants had it just as bad.'

HOUSE PRICES STILL RISING

by our housing correspondent, Des Res

In the time it has taken you to read this sentence, average house prices in Northern Ireland have increased by £250,000. 'It's great news for anyone selling their property,' local estate agent William Joyce told our reporter yesterday. 'Of course, then they have to buy another place to live, which makes the price increase completely meaningless.'

'Still it's definitely great news for estate agents,' added Mr Joyce, 'and that's the main thing.'

World of Loyalism

- The **UVF** has announced it will not be destroying any more mobile phone masts, after thousands of people were unable to text in their drug orders.

- The **Ulster Paramilitary Research Group** has lost its status as an umbrella organisation. 'To qualify as an umbrella,' explained an Oxford English Dictionary spokesman yesterday, 'it must cover at least one person.'

- The **UDA** has been criticised by other loyalists for issuing a fund-raising 2003 calendar. 'Nobody in the UDA needs this year's calendar,' said a UVF spokesman.

IRA STATEMENT CLEARS THE AIR

by our republican correspondent, Anne Phoblacht

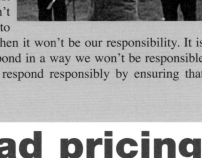

The IRA has issued a historic New Year Statement outlining its historic vision for the peace process in the historic months ahead. 'They aren't historic months yet, of course,' explained a Sinn Fein spokesman yesterday, 'but they will be just as soon as they've happened.'

IRA New Year Statement in full

'Everybody has a responsibility not to act irresponsibly. We support peace, so anyone irresponsible enough not to support us doesn't support peace. If others don't support peace it could force us to respond. But we don't want to respond, so if there is a response then it won't be our responsibility. It is everyone else's responsibility to ensure that we don't have to respond in a way we won't be responsible for, so the two governments have a particular responsibility to respond responsibly by ensuring that everyone else understands their responsibilities.'

P. O'Neill

JOHN POPPER'S ARDOYNE/ GLENBRYN DICTIONARY

It's themmuns fault, so it is!
I must question the motivations of the other tradition.

Police brutalitay!
I have been prevented from starting a riot.

This cammunitay is under siege
If I had any intention of going to work I would be unable to do so.

My nerves iz wracked, so they are
It is not my fault that I am drunk at 10 a.m.

What abowt aaar human rights?
I am entitled to break the law whenever I feel like it.

Them camaras isn't fur!
How can I start a riot with those things watching me?

I'm a cammunitay raprasantative
I'm a bigoted old slapper with nothing to offer except hatred.

Road pricing for town?

by our transport correspondent, Fred Petrolhead

Portadown Borough Council is considering London-style road pricing for the town. Under the proposal, motorists will be paid £5 a day to drive into a central zone. The scheme will be funded by ripping up railway lines and selling them off for script.

'Please, please, please come shopping in Portadown,' said a council spokesman yesterday. 'We've got a McDonalds and everything.'

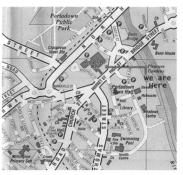

Drug-drive test unveiled

by our crime correspondent, Rob Berry

The PSNI has revealed details of its new roadside drug test, to be rolled up across the province later this year.

'Suspicious drivers will be stopped and offered a pint of vodka,' explained officer Bill Mason to our reporter yesterday. 'Anyone who says "I'm sorry, that ruins my pill" will be taken in for further questioning.'

All aboard famine ship!

by our Irish history correspondent, A. Mone

Replica Irish famine ship the Moaning Johnson has docked in Belfast to pick up a cross-community crew of disadvantaged young people [TM], before sailing on to America. The vessel's mission is to build reconciliation between Protestants and Catholics through the healing power of anti-English historical grievances.

'Taking these kids away will help bring peace to Belfast,' a project spokesman told our reporter yesterday, 'at least until Easter, when I'm afraid we'll have to bring them back again.'

8:00 Miss Marple Investigates

When a choirboy is crushed by a falling organ, Miss Marple performs a low-level scan of the vicar's hard-drive.

7:00 Stars up their Stars

A glittering panel of celebrity guests sit around wondering who'll be arrested next.

9:00 The Who Unplugged

Exclusive footage of the empty wall-socket behind Pete Townshend's computer desk.

CHESTNUT LODGE

Plywood homes for the incredibly stupid

The Atlantis

Floods every year
Ideal for yachtsman

The Beckham

Blindingly expensive
Completely tasteless

The Bridget Jones

Die alone
Be eaten by your cat

The Dealer

Because nobody with an honest job could possibly afford it

The Portadown News

BBC RADIO BLUSTER

Seamus Austin talks to Sinn Fein's Kerry Jelly

(followed by Sectarian Thought for the Day)

Seamus: 'So why were you spying on community workers?'

Kerry: 'Look! Look! Seamus, the question you need to ask yourself here is why the RUC-PSNI told the media.'

Seamus: 'Why shouldn't they have told the media?'

Kerry: 'Because! Because! Because they're just doing it to undermine the peace process!'

Seamus: 'Isn't spying on community workers undermining the peace process?'

Kerry: 'Only if people find out! Can't you see the timing of this is very suspicious?'

Seamus: 'When would have been a good time?'

Kerry: 'Look! Look! That question has been deliberately timed to undermine the peace process . . . .'

. . . continued until enough people wise up

DUP welcomes mosque

by our religious affairs correspondent, Helen Brimstone

DUP councillor Marvin Currie has welcomed plans to build a mosque in Portadown.

'Free Presbyterians and Muslims have a great deal in common,' councillor Currie told our reporter yesterday. 'We're both obsessed with sex and alcohol, treat women like we own them, talk a load of nonsense about Israel and let our preachers mix with terrorists. I reckon they'll fit right in.'

LOCAL BOYS HEAD FOR IRAQ

by our security correspondent, Roger Base

Hundreds of local Royal Irish Regiment soldiers are saying a tearful goodbye to their 15-year-old girlfriends this weekend

as they head off for the Persian Gulf.

'There's some guy with a beard we're supposed to kill and apparently it's all a bit dodgy,' one squaddie told our reporter yesterday. 'So really, it'll be just like old times.'

'Give My Head Spotlight'

by our television correspondent, Andy Flicker

An internal BBC investigation is underway after Tuesday's episode of 'Spotlight' turned out to be ten times funnier than Friday's episode of 'Give My Head Peace'.

'The whole country was in stitches watching Sammy Duddy's wife saying "You've killed my Chihuahua ya bastards!" and John White screaming "You're taking my handicrafts out of context",' explained a BBC spokesman yesterday. 'Meanwhile, laughter has to be piped in to the Give My Head Peace studios from old people's homes as far away as Belleek.'

'Prods and taigs, ha ha ha,' said a Give My Head Peace scriptwriter this morning. 'You know, Prods and taigs, ha ha ha.'

BBC RADIO BLUSTER

Seamus Austin talks to DUP councillor Paul Dingleberry
(followed by Sectarian Thought for the Day)

Dingleberry: These inquiries are a concession to terrorists. What about the innocent victims?

Austin: You mean, like Robert Hamill?

Dingleberry: No! I mean Protestant victims.

Austin: You mean, like Billy Wright?

Dingleberry: Yes

Austin: But wasn't he a terrorist?

Dingleberry: Look! You don't understand! THEM FENIANS GETS EVERYTHING.

(continued around in circles for the rest of our lives)

Ferry in safety drama

by our shipping correspondent, Lloyd Bridges

B&O Ferries has suspended sailings to Scotland after an incident on Wednesday night. 'We'd just left port when the vessel developed an alarming list to the extreme right,' explained a spokesman for the famous sea-company.

'The crew discovered 50 fat people wearing heavy gold jewellery sitting in the starboard lounge. When we told them they'd have to move for safety reasons, one of them said, "Oh God, not again".'

New twist to carpet feud

by our feud correspondent, Billy Shootspatrick

There were dramatic developments in Portadown's bitter carpet feud this week, as Ulster Discount Axminster warned its rivals that 'We won't be beaten on price'. 'There's no skirting around it,' said PSNI officer Bill Mason yesterday. 'They've got the competition completely floored.'

Local residents have expressed their cynicism at the development. 'It's just the same old pattern we've always had,' one told our reporter. 'At the end of the day, all any of these guys are interested in is selling rugs.'

JOHN WHITE'S
'handicrafts taken out of context'

Hand-stitched souvenir wallet

MORE SLIPPERY EXCUSES

by our weather correspondent, Windy Miller

Stormont officials have apologised for this week's traffic chaos, after roads were blanketed in up to 0.00005 inches of slush.

'The Northern Ireland Office does not believe in using grit to solve our problems,' explained a spokesman yesterday. 'The best way of dealing with dangerous conditions is just to sit around hoping for a bit of a thaw.'

DODGY BANKS HIT BANK

by our business correspondent, Reg Empty

First Ulster Northern has hit back at comments by the Consumer's Association that local banks are 'stuck in the last century'.

'We are stuck in the last century,' admitted a bank official yesterday. 'But the rest of Northern Ireland is stuck in the 17th century, so actually we're 300 years ahead.'

(There was a charge of £15 for this article.)

Your complete guide to 'Acts of Completion'

- London to demand complete decommissioning
- Dublin to demand complete disbandment
- Washington to demand complete co-operation over policing
- Unionists to be completely demanding
- Sinn Fein to completely ignore the lot of them

This week's bomb attack in Enniskillen was provoked by the large number of security force personnel in the area. The enforcement of law and order throughout Fermanagh has reached unacceptable levels, especially at polling stations. The police must prevent further incidents by not trying to prevent them.

Michelle Gildernew MP

TOWN TO GET ITS HOLE?

by our business correspondent, Reg Empty

DUP councillors are opposing plans for a £500 million lignite mine and power station outside Ballymoney.

'There'll be no strip mining in this town,' councillor Marvin Currie told our reporter yesterday, 'especially for "dirty coal", and I don't like the sound of this word "ore" either.'

Councillor Currie also claimed that mining operations will lead to 'devil music and fornication', although this is believed to be a misunderstanding over the term 'bedrock'.

Have you tried the Michelle Gildernew Diet?????

If you're shocked by how much weight you've put on lately, why not blame the food? If the food hadn't been there, you wouldn't have eaten it, so it's not your fault at all. Good luck!

Michelle xxx

south AYRSHIRE

A Special Ulster-Scots Welcome to our Lower Shankill Visitors

"Gae Hame Ye Bampots"

doktormoog@hotmail.com

Our Wee Jeffrey

2003　　www.PortadownNews.com

LAST CHANCE TO SEE . . .

by our science correspondent, Bunsen Burns

STARGAZERS are watching the nebulous cluster this weekend as the Ulster Unionist Planet makes its closest approach to Earth for 60,000 years.

'Because of its eccentric orbit, this planet is usually too dim to be noticeable,' explained a spokesman for South Armagh Observatory yesterday, 'however it's currently making an astronomical show of itself.'

The Ulster Unionist Planet will be visible at twilight for several more months, before being permanently eclipsed.

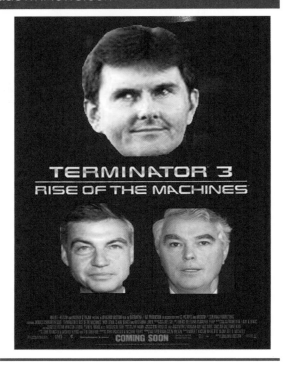

DERAILMENT 'COULD HAVE BEEN AVOIDED' SHOCK

Grudgie
The UUP Election Helicopter

'Come on, Grudgie!' said all the other little helicopters. 'You have to fly David Trimble to Stormont!'

'But I don't want to go to Stormont,' said Grudgie, 'and if I don't go, then neither can anybody else.'

Then all the other little helicopters cried, because Grudgie was being a selfish bastard.

Joint plan rolled out

by our unionist correspondent, Will March

JEFFREY DONALDSON and Sir Reg Empey are considering a joint bid for the leadership of the Ulster Unionist Party.

Should they succeed, Northern Ireland will have a First Minister, a Second First Minister and a Deputy First Minister, compelling the SDLP to appoint a Second Deputy First Minister. This means the former Office of the First and Deputy First Ministers will be known as the Office of the First, Second, Deputy and Second Deputy First Ministers.

'The beauty of this plan is its simplicity,' said a Unionist spokesman yesterday.

Jeffrey attends burial

by our unionist correspondent, Will March

Jeffrey Donaldson is now expected to attend the funeral of the Ulster Unionist Party, which will finally be buried later this month after almost thirty years of digging its own grave.

Five foot under

'We're really glad that Jeffrey will be there,' said a spokesman for the unionist family yesterday. 'After all, it was his tireless campaigning that made this possible.'

Donaldson explains his position

My party's defeat is a victory for me

Christmas party warning

by our unionist correspondent, **Will March**

Health officials are advising people to behave sensibly at parties during the festive period.

"It is easy to get carried away and make a fool of yourself by being rude to colleagues, ignoring company policy or even standing on a chair and shouting 'I'm the boss! I'm the boss!' until everybody tells you to shut up," warned a spokesman yesterday.

"Worse still, some people then go on to another party and do it all over again. Our advice, if you think you might be about to make a fool of yourself this year, is to organise a little party for yourself and a couple of friends that nobody else will ever hear about."

Robert McCartney QC was unavailable for comment.

POLICE SERVICE of NORTHERN IRELAND

APOLOGY

I'M VERY VERY VERY SORRY FOR STATING THE BLEEDIN' OBVIOUS

Lost and Found

Found
18 pipe bombs
Lost
18 lives in the past two years

BBC

Street Detectives

Gosh, wasn't it fun that time the golf club organised a treasure hunt? Could we use that idea? It's been done already? OK, let's just show some people driving around aimlessly meeting local 'characters'. Will that do? Super!

Thinking about a new car?

Why not visit The Odyssey car park – hundreds of models to choose from.

Catholic man not shot

by our loyalist correspondent, Billy Shootspatrick

A 26-year-old Catholic man has not been shot dead in North Belfast.

Brendan Lawson was walking down the Ardoyne Road at 4 p.m. yesterday when two shots did not ring out, not hitting him in the head and neck and not killing him instantly. The UDA is believed to be responsible.

'Gosh, well done guys,' Insecurity Minister Jane Kennedy told a packed press conference this morning, 'Have a f***ing biscuit.'

Those shock Portadown News Poll results in full

ARE YOU PROTESTANT?

Protestants: 100%

ARE YOU CATHOLIC?

Catholics: 100%

Pipe bombs for peace

by our loyalist correspondent, Billy Shootspatrick

The UDA pipe bombs abandoned in West Belfast this week are to be made into a cross-community peace sculpture. Arts Council chiefs have commissioned a team of loyalist ex-prisoners to work on the £500,000 project, provisionally entitled 'Some Pipe Bombs Welded Together, Like'.

'We expect to find a home for them in Larne,' explained an Arts Council spokesman yesterday, 'seeing as they'd have ended up in homes in Larne anyway.'

Celebrations on Rathlin!

by our offshore island correspondent, Aaron Sweater

Rathlin Island residents will soon have sectarianism on tap thanks to the construction of a £10-million bigotry pipeline, which will deliver fresh hot and cold running bigotry directly into homes. Until now islanders have had to fetch their bigotry from private wells of bitterness.

'Finally we can enjoy the same quality of life as everyone else in Northern Ireland,' one local man told our reporter yesterday. 'Maybe next year we'll get electricity as well. Then we can really get wired into each other.'

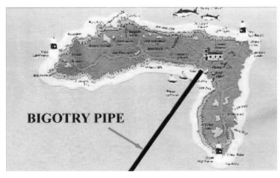

BIGOTRY PIPE

US in 'Twits Out' shock

by our American correspondent, Brad Cheeseburger

Bernadette McAliskey has been refused permission to enter the United States, in a move many commentators are calling 'the worst human rights atrocity in the history of the world'.

'Look, it's quite simple really,' explained a US immigration official yesterday. 'Everybody we don't like gets told to leave the country. How could any Irish Republican complain about that?'

SPOT THE DIFFERENCE

by our religious affairs correspondent, Helen Brimstone

This year's Ash Wednesday celebrations have passed off without major incident, despite most of the province's Catholic population effectively tattooing 'Yes, I'm a fenian' on their foreheads.

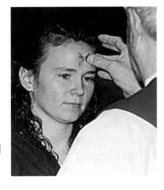

'This may be a sign of progress,' one local priest told our reporter yesterday, 'or it may mean most Protestants still think "Ash" is a band from Downpatrick.'

The Portadown News

11TH MARCH 2003   www.PortadownNews.com

Agreement to disagree agreed

by our agreement correspondent, B. Onduse

The pro-Agreement parties have announced a historic agreement to disagree, but have agreed to postpone making their agreement public so as not to undermine their public positions on the Agreement.

Republicans have agreed to accuse pro-Agreement unionists of agreeing with anti-Agreement unionists, although Unionists have disagreed over how to accuse Sinn Fein of not agreeing with the Agreement.

The agreement to disagree will remain in force until an election date is agreed, after which pro-Agreement parties will agree to agree while anti-Agreement parties will disagree with everyone. Prime Minister Tony Blair described the two-day Agreement talks as 'agreeably agreeable'.

On the runs?

Those new sanctions in full

Sinn Fein will be fined every time Gerry Adams uses the following phrases:

'The reality is . . .'	£50
'You'll have to ask the IRA about that'	£100
'It now falls to the British Government to . . .'	£250
'. . . and the media also has a responsibility to . . .'	£500
'Agus, agus, errrr . . .'	£1,000
'The onus is now on . . .'	£2,000
'Everyone must realise that . . .'	£5,000
'Look. The reality is . . .'	expulsion

Northern Ireland CRIMESTOPPERS
13:21 04.03.2003

● Were you in Hillsborough recently?
● Did you see either of these men acting suspiciously in the vicinity of the Castle?
● The Police (and everyone else) would like to find out what they are up to.

doktormoog@hotmail.com

Truth Commission setback

by our justice correspondent, Gerry Rumpole

The Chief Constable's proposal for a South African-style Truth and Reconciliation Commission has been dropped.

'We don't think it would work in Northern Ireland,' a Government spokesman told our reporter yesterday. 'There just aren't enough black people.'

Aff t' jail wi' yu laddie

by our Ulster-Scots correspondent, **Jock Grant**

The Ulster-Scots Agency has been found guilty of language abuse.

'This is one of the most disgusting cases I've ever heard,' judge John Pepper told the Agency yesterday. 'You kidnapped innocent words under false pretences, then horribly mutilated them for your own cynical purposes. I sentence you to £4 million a year of community funding.'

PANIC IN DUNDALK

by our security correspondent, *Roger Base*

There was panic in Dundalk on Friday morning after radio reports that British troops had crossed the border.

'I didn't realise Iraq had a border as well,' one confused resident told our reporter yesterday. 'Which side do you go to for the cheap petrol?'

PORTADOWN'S FAVOURITE COLUMNISTS!

Judith Collins

How ironic that David Trimble supports America's invasion of Iraq, while at the same time asking Gerry Adams to say 'The War is Over' here in Northern Ireland.

Don't the little children of Iraq deserve peace too?

I was at a dinner party in South Belfast last weekend . . . etc.

Steven Queen

How ironic that Gerry Adams opposes America's liberation of Iraq, while at the same time refusing to tell David Trimble that 'The War is Over' here in Northern Ireland.

Don't the little children of Iraq deserve freedom too?

I was at a dinner party in South Belfast last weekend . . . etc.

Poyntzpass murderers in moving apology

We are both very very sorry that we were caught

Portadown News
JobSeeker

Staff required

Library Security Guard

(may suit former ambulance driver)

Decommissioning

Water Service to decommission pipes

by our decommissioning correspondent, B. Onduse

The Water Service is to put its entire distribution network 'permanently and verifiably beyond use'.

"As the recent outbreak of Loyalist violence has shown, pipes are deadly weapons," explained Water Service Chief Executive Brendan Widebore yesterday. "In order to move the peace process forward, we've contacted the International Commission on Decommissioning with a series of proposals to take the pipe permanently out of Irish politics.'

The Portadown News understands that the various decommissioning 'modalities' on offer include: Filling with concrete; Explosion; Dumping at sea; or Privatisation. "It's true that our proposals will leave the public without a water supply," admits Mr Widebore. "Still, we all knew that peace would come at a price."

SDLP bases to close?

by our security correspondent, Roger Base

The police have recommended that SDLP bases across the country be closed down.

'Although there was a need for the SDLP during the troubles, there's no real point to them any more,' explained PSNI officer Bill Mason yesterday.

Sinn Fein has reacted angrily to the proposal. 'Closing down the SDLP was our idea,' said a party spokesman yesterday. 'The PSNI should get some policies of their own.'

Police station decommissioned

by our security correspondent, Roger Base

As part of its commitments under the Weston Park Talks, the government has announced that Portadown Police Station is to be demolished.

"The removal of this fortress of British oppression will be welcomed by all the people of Edward Street," said local Sinn Fein Councillor Brendan McKenna, "who have been concerned for many years that I might leave another car bomb outside it."

After demolition, the site will be occupied by a Memorial Peace Garden. Anyone wishing to report a crime should write to Brice Dickson at the Northern Ireland Human Rights Commission, who will send them a standard letter explaining why it's all society's fault.

SHAMROCK CELEBRATIONS IN US

by our American correspondent, Brad Cheeseburger

Local politicians have flown to Washington to remind America that Northern Ireland is still the centre of the universe.

'I have a dream,' President George W. Bush told reporters, 'that one day little Protestant children and little Kurdish children will play together in the streets of Ulsterland. That's why I'm giving Adams Hussein until St Patrick's Day to decommission his weapons.'

Gerry Adams marked the occasion by turning a traditional shade of green.

Adams asks wife to do dishes

by our paramilitary correspondent, P. O'Neill

In a historic move for which we should all be extremely grateful, Sinn Fein President Gerry Adams has asked his wife to do the dishes.

"While the important thing is that the dishes are in the sink," Mr Adams told a packed press conference yesterday, "the time has come to put them in the cupboard."

However doubts remain as to exactly when Mrs Adams will wash the dishes.

"I am not my wife, although I do have some influence over her decisions," explained Mr Adams. "She could do the dishes straight away, or she could say, 'Do them yourself, you beardie bastard, sure you've never done an honest day's work in your life.'"

Local heroes hunt Hussein

by every local newspaper in Northern Ireland

Soldiers from Portadown are amongst the British troops seeing active service in Iraq this weekend.

'We're here to do a job and we're keen to get the job done,' local man Private (INSERT NAME) told our reporter yesterday, via the Ministry of Defence Press Office.

'We've trained for the job and we'll finish the job,' added Private (INSERT NAME), 'because at the end of the day being a soldier is more than just a job.'

Private (INSERT NAME) yesterday

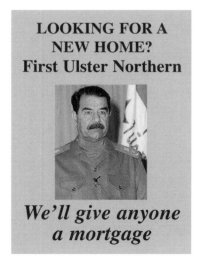
'YES, IT'S NO'
SAY SINN FEIN
by our republican correspondent, Anne Phoblacht

Sinn Fein will not join the policing board until it joins the policing board, Gerry Adams told his party's annual conference this weekend.

'There can be no policing without republican support, so until the police have republican support then republicans cannot support the police,' Mr Adams informed cheering volunteers yesterday, adding, 'This decision is final until we change it.'

Questioned later by the media, North Belfast MLA Gerry Kelly said, 'You have the right to remain silent.'

International Headlines
Trimble backs war
'That's me fked then', admits Saddam (see page 42)**

(see page 42)

Adams opposes war
'That's me fked then', admits Saddam (see page 42)**

(see page 42)

Communiqué to the Northern Ireland political parties from President George W. Bush

Get on with it W.

BACKHAND COMPLIMENT
by our corruption correspondent, Bungdit Singh

Nationalist politicians have welcomed this week's damning reports into corruption at LEDU and fraudulent payments to landowners.

'Northern Ireland gets more like the Republic every day,' said an SDLP spokesman yesterday.

We gotta mop up these pockets of resistance

PORTADOWN NEWS
INFOBOX

This week: how destroying an SDLP councillor's car will bring about a united Ireland

1. Councillor has to get the bus
2. Councillor misses policing board meeting
3. Police Service collapses without SDLP support
4. Community demands help from dissident republicans
5. Continuity IRA establishes popular government
6. All-Ireland socialist paradise declared

Next week: how shooting a Chihuahua secures the union

Travel News

New Derry Trains unveiled

END OF THE LINE FOR NIR?

by our security correspondent, Roger Base

The Government is planning to disband the NIR, security sources have warned, claiming that it is an obstacle to 'moving things forward'.

'Some of the better-trained personnel may be stationed in Germany but everyone else will just have to change,' explained a Government spokesman yesterday, 'probably at Lisburn.'

Unionist politicians have expressed outrage at the proposals. 'We'll be asking the government to examine a number of points,' said local councillor Marvin Currie. 'They must provide a level crossing field before de-siding anything.'

What's Up Portadown!

ARTS & ENTERTAINMENT

AMATEUR BOXING
Country Fried Chicken, High Street
Some Twat in a Band Uniform vs.
Some Other Twat in a Band Uniform.
Every Friday & Saturday night.

Pollution Heritage Trail
Lough Neagh Discovery Centre
Learn about Kinnego Bay, where dead sheep,
Buckfast pee and the stuff even May Pork throws
away combine in some of the most interesting
chemistry this side of Jupiter.
Includes video presentation:
"The Life-Cycle of the Shopping Trolley".

Inspirational Praise Tent Mission
The Foot-and-Mouth Exclusion Zone, Annaghmore
American preacher Brad Cheeseburger delivers his
uplifting message: "Rejoice in the damnation of
thine enemies."
The Lord Shall Provide. Tea & Biscuits.

Sectarian Rioting (Semi-Finals)
Craigwell Avenue
Tough refereeing will be needed as Corcrain
Drunken Losers take on Ballyoran Hopeless
Chuckies. Which one of these two young teams
will make it to July's decider?
B.Y.O.B.

Paintings By Numbers
The Library Gallery
Thatched cottages, rolling mists, kittens in a basket.
Warning: Artist may be present.

Back Entry Drama Society Presents
"Bigots at Bedtime"
Portadown Town Hall
Laugh along as our society's hopeless divisions are
gently alluded to – though hardly criticised – with
third-rate sexual innuendo.
Protestant Audience Night: Friday.
Catholic Audience Night: Tuesday.

Fashion
LOOKING GOOD THIS SUMMER!

It's our new fashion column, with Sean-Paul Goatier

With the promise of warmer days, the good people of Portadown will soon be paying a little more attention to their appearance. And not before time! To help you look good this summer, the Portadown News has compiled this handy cut-out-and-keep guide to common fashion mistakes in the Greater Craigavon metropolitan area.

LEISUREWEAR ON FAT PEOPLE
Nothing clashes with a tracksuit like clinical obesity. If your idea of sporting activity is passing your chips around at the match, better go buy yourself a nice baggy t-shirt.

RANGERS SHIRTS ON MEN
To you, a harmless gesture of allegiance; to everyone else, a declaration of mindless bigotry. Take a tip from our Catholic neighbours: you don't see them down town on a Saturday afternoon in their Celtic tops, now do you?

RANGERS SHIRTS ON WOMEN
There's no hope for you. Try not to travel between Corcrain and Jameson's during daylight hours.

TINTED WINDOWS ON A VAUXHALL CORSA
Oh dear, oh dear. Still a virgin, aren't you son? I'm afraid that time you shot your load over Shelley-Anne McAvoy's leg behind The Coach doesn't count. (Except maybe to her.) Why not just spray-paint "I'm a Virgin" on your rear spoiler? It sends the same message as tinted windows, but does less damage to the re-sale value.

TATTOOS ON MEN
Fashionable now, but what about in 20 years' time, when everybody's Dad's got one? Didn't think of that, eh, did you?

TATTOOS ON WOMEN
The message your tattoo sends to prospective partners is: "I'm desperate to fit in, have no self-respect, will fuck you on the first date, and am the precise opposite of what you're looking for in a serious relationship." Good luck with the rest of your life, dear.

The Portadown News

8TH APRIL 2003 · www.PortadownNews.com

Good news for Larne!

by our American correspondent, Brad Cheeseburger

AMERICAN President George W. Bush arrives in Northern Ireland this week for a series of meetings aimed at resolving the Larne Special Olympics scandal.

"We realise people in Larne were disappointed when the Iraqi team pulled out," explained a White House spokesman yesterday, "which is why we're doing all we can to create as many disabled Iraqis as possible."

Crippling blow for Larne

by our Larne correspondent, Billy Shootspatrick

LARNE has pulled out of the Catholic Olympics due to continued hostilities in the County Antrim town.

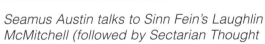

"We're all very disappointed," explained team captain Father Pat Wilson yesterday, "but it would be wrong to leave while our people are under attack."

BBC RADIO BLUSTER

Seamus Austin talks to Sinn Fein's Laughlin McMitchell (followed by Sectarian Thought for the Day)

Laughlin: Plastic bullets must be banned now.

Seamus: But the police say they need more time.

Laughlin: There's no excuse for having these weapons!

Seamus: So they should be immediately decommissioned?

Laughlin: Yes. What? No. Hang on. Injustice! Injustice!

(continued until the emergency Ard Fheis)

Portadown News Homebuyer

A 12-page glossy colour supplement featuring luxury homes in ideal locations which you can read while sitting in your

pokey living room, becoming lost for a moment in the fantasy that you too might aspire to such a lifestyle, before the dream is shattered by an obscenity shouted outside your front window

by one of the feral urchins who have rendered your own house completely worthless.

BRUTALITY COMPLAINT

by our policing correspondent, Roz Peeler

There have been complaints about brutality at this week's anti-war protest in Belfast city centre.

'I'm not surprised,' PSNI Officer Bill Mason told our reporter yesterday. 'Bernadette McAliskey was brutal in 1969 and she's still brutal today. Some things never change.'

IT'S 'SHOP THE WAR'

by our anti-war correspondent, Grant Dole

'STOP THE WAR' campaigners say they were delighted with the success of this Tuesday's protest at Sprucefield.

'It was an ideal location,' one told our reporter yesterday. 'Only at Sprucefield can you combine the fight against American imperialism with the convenience of late-night shopping at wholesale prices.'

Saddam Hussein in Saddam Hussein shock?

PORTADOWN'S FAVOURITE COLUMNISTS!

Judith Collins

HYPOCRISY! How can Bush ask us to make peace while making war in Iraq?

Steven Queen

HYPOCRISY! How can Bush ask us to surrender while fighting terrorism in Iraq?

Julian Simmons

HYPOCRISY! How can Steve try to win Karen back after sleeping with Janice?

IRA issues clear statement

Clear off

EERIE HUSH FALLS OVER CITY

by our security correspondent, Roger Base

An eerie silence hangs over the streets of Belfast today, as thousands of anti-war protestors sulk indoors.

Sources indicate most have gone home for the weekend, where their mums have promised to cook them a nice Sunday lunch while their dads laugh quietly at them from behind the newspaper.

'Saddam may be gone, but it changes nothing,' one angry protestor told our reporter yesterday. 'I'm still a pompous little moron riddled with acne and self-hatred.'

COLLUSION OUTRAGE SCANDAL!

Only in today's Portadown News, it's your own cut-out-and-keep Loyalist collusion info-graphic

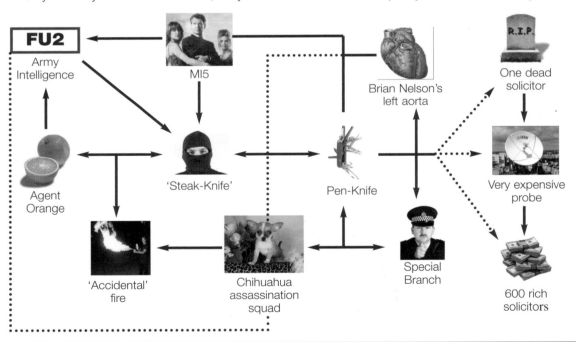

CAR CRASH IN DERRY

Sinn Fein demands collision inquiry

Full story page 42

DUP demands answers

by our security correspondent, Roger Base

The Democratic Unionist Party has demanded an immediate public inquiry into security force collusion during the 1980s.

'These allegations raise important questions that must be answered,' said a DUP spokesman yesterday. 'Specifically, if there was a huge government conspiracy to murder Catholics, why are there still so many of them?'

SARS FEAR CANCELS ELECTIONS

by our health correspondent, Angela Crippen

Next month's crucial Stormont elections have been cancelled due to fears of a SARS epidemic, the Portadown News can exclusively reveal.

SARS (Shinner Assembly Results Syndrome) mostly affects the young, sick and vulnerable and has already caused several fatalities.

'Elections are off until we find a cure,' explained a Northern Ireland Office spokesman yesterday. 'We can't risk spreading this contagion any further.'

Blair's three questions

Leaked exclusively to all newspapers

The Portadown News has obtained this transcript of Tony Blair's three direct questions to the republican movement, along with Sinn Fein's replies.

Did you have a good weekend?
Sinn Fein believes that everyone on this island has the right to a good weekend.

What's your favourite film?
Sinn Fein believes that all films have equal status under the terms of the Good Friday Agreement.

Do you like ice-cream?
Sinn Fein believes that ice-cream is best enjoyed within an all-Ireland context.

Understanding North Belfast

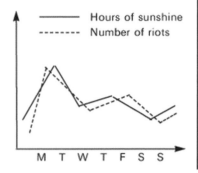

- —— Hours of sunshine
- ------ Number of riots

M T W T F S S

Sparks fly at NIE

by our business correspondent, Reg Empty

Northern Ireland Electricity has warned that any further attacks on its staff could have serious consequences.

'The current situation is shocking,' said an NIE spokesman yesterday. 'We're calling on those with connections to provide a lead.'

McGuinness: the Downing St ears

by our republican correspondent, Anne Phoblacht

The Portadown News has obtained this exclusive transcript of Martin McGuinness's conversation with Downing Street's Chief Policy Advisor Jonathan Powell.

MM: I hate that unionist ass Willie Thompson.

JP: Yeah, he's an ass.

MM: Just like Jeffrey Donaldson, Roy Beggs, Clifford Forsyth, Martin Smyth . . .

JP: Hey! Don't list them all, as if you thought this conversation was being recorded and could be used later on to embarrass me.

MM: OK, but we both hate unionists don't we?

JP: Yes, we English have so much in common with you Irish.

MM: Indeed – perhaps we should form some sort of 'union'.

STOP PRESS: Portadown News journalist Anne Phoblacht has been arrested under Section 42 of the Secret Officials Act.

Electoral Office
Northern Ireland

No Card
No Vote
No Election

Speak Sinn Fein!

It's the language everyone's having to learn

This week's verb:
'To decommission'

■ We won't decommission	tense past
■ We can't decommission	verbal (intransigent)
■ We might decommission	singular provonoun
■ We should decommission	slang (Brit.)
■ We will decommission	tense present
■ We have decommissioned	perfect future

Export success for UDA

by our business correspondent, Reg Empty

LOCAL business development agency InvestNI has praised the UDA for this week's shooting in Manchester.

'It's always good to see a local company get a mainland contract,' said a spokesman yesterday.

ARMY LEARNS GAELIC!

by our GAA correspondent, Sam O'McGuire

The British Army's GAA team is to play a historic game against long-term rivals Crossmaglen. The Army's GAA squad comprises 15 players plus an unknown number of informers.

'I'm confident we'll beat our opponents,' Lt Julian Sandhurst told our reporter yesterday, 'as shooting them is now considered inappropriate.'

Balmoral Show Winners

| Total Bull | Biggest Cow | Loudest Runt |

ROBINSON IN 'Am I party leader yet?' shock

It's time for a FAIR DEAL

Did you just hear a 'click'?

BIOTERRORISM: PUBLIC NOTICE

Residents of Northern Ireland are reminded that laughing at the Government's obvious double-standard on terrorism will only increase your risk of ingesting any anthrax we've released.

Travel News

Train drivers target vandals

by our security correspondent, Roger Base

This is Northern Ireland Railways' latest weapon against vandalism. The German-built 'Mucker-Fokker' rail-mounted cannon was purchased following last weekend's stone-throwing incident at Great Victoria Street Station, when a brick narrowly missed killing a female train driver – and injuring dozens of passengers.

"The Mucker-Fokker cannon fires twelve 8-inch high-explosive shells per minute," explained a Translink spokesman, "delivering effective youth crime prevention up to a range of three miles."

Summer/Autumn firing timetables are available free from all main-line stations. A machine-gun substitution service may operate on Sundays.

New Citybus vehicles

The Ardoyne Flyer

The Strangford College Smoker

The Short Strand Shopper

Train crash horror

by our transport correspondent, Fred Petrolhead

TELEVISION executives have expressed their horror at the poor quality of video footage from this week's North Coast train crash.

"Obviously we were delighted when we heard that a passenger had recorded the entire incident," TV producer Andrew Ghoul told our reporter yesterday. "I immediately commissioned six new episodes of our popular series 'When Trains Hit Landslides', plus an entirely new series called 'When Landslides Hit Trains'."

"So you can imagine my disappointment," added Mr Ghoul, "when the video turned out to be just a bunch of pensioners standing around suffering from shock. Really, some people have no consideration for the needs of factual television."

Lookalikes

Sue Ramsey in 'Jabba the Hutt' shock

Scappaticci in Hugo Duncan shock

Brice Dickson in Lloyd Grossman shock

Sue Ramsey in Fra McCann shock

The Portadown News

20TH MAY 2003 — www.PortadownNews.com

WHO IS THE REAL STAKEKNIFE?

by our allegation correspondent, D. Niall

As disputes rage over the identity of the IRA double-agent known as Stakeknife, we take a closer look at the leading suspects

Bernie 'Needles' Needham
Ran the IRA's notorious 'Knitting Squad', responsible for some of the worst balaclavas of the troubles.

Niccolo Machiavelli
Renaissance Italian philosopher whose writing acknowledged the cynical realities of state power. Now runs a chip-shop in Poleglass.

Hong Kong Phooey
An important crime-fighting asset during the last 1970s. Could be Henry, the mild-mannered janitor, or possibly Rosemary, the telephone operator.

Martin McGuinness
Definitely not Stakeknife – but wouldn't it be fun if he was?

Portrush latest:
Windfarm plan outrage

Ballymoney latest:
Lignite mine outrage

Stormont latest:
Power-sharing still off

Maskey 'failure' – DUP

by our local government correspondent, David Rottenborough

Alex Maskey's tenure as Mayor has been 'a massive disappointment', claim the DUP.

'Maskey's total failure to do anything provocative was clearly provocative,' explained a party spokesman yesterday, adding, 'I have nothing to add.'

GRAFTING RECRUITMENT
Leaving the RIR? We have 6,000 vacancies:

| Bouncers | Security Guards | Bar Staff | Loyalists |

Unemployment latest:
Carpet factory job cuts leave shop-floor bare

See page 42

The Belfast
Telegraph

The recent fire at our Royal Avenue office gives us yet another excuse to publish a photo of a semi-clad girl. This is sexy firegirl Sue Mammary (19) from Antrim.

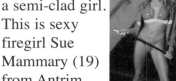

'I wanna hold your hand'

by our republican correspondent, Anne Phoblacht

Gerry Adams has offered to reach out his hand to Protestants, having wiped most of the blood off earlier. His cross-community confidence-building proposals include:

- Adams to personally explain why Unionism is 'stupid'
- IRA to 'sincerely forgive' its victims
- Protestants to be issued with 'Right to Remain' certificates (valid until Easter 2016)

GET IN. GET OUT. GET EVEN.

MARK WAHLBERG
CHARLIZE THERON
EDWARD NORTON
THE ITALIAN JOB

Tory commits political suicide

BANG!

Election protest

by our election correspondent, Sir Robin Someday

Hundreds of Sinn Fein voters have protested across West Belfast at the cancelling of the Stormont elections.

The protestors then swapped passports, boarded a fleet of black taxis and protested in North Belfast as well.

ONE A-MAZING DAY OUT!

by our republican correspondent, Anne Phoblacht

Republican prisoners welfare group Coiste has published its proposals for a museum on the site of the Maze prison. Visitor attractions will include:

- **Hunger Strike café**
- **Mass Breakout souvenir shop**
- **Dirty Protest bouncy castle**
- **Strip-search club (with lock-ins)**
- **David Ervine meditation garden**

Asked what members had learned from their own time inside the Maze, a Coiste spokesman said, 'You're only gay if you take it.'

'Best Kept' awards

by our floral correspondent, Gerry Anium

ANDERSONSTOWN has won this year's Best Kept Large Secret Award.

Presenting the coveted prize, the judges commended the district for its 'Colourful arrangements, perennial greenery and imaginative use of plants'.

More new Fionnualas

by our Fionola correspondent,
Finula Fionnula

THE CATHOLIC NAMES COUNCIL has approved another 16 official spellings of 'Fionula', including a phonetic 'Finoola', an Ulster-Scots 'Fainoughla' and a standardised European 'Finneaula'.

'This will improve choice for parents,' explained a spokesman yesterday, 'as well as confusing Protestants.'

A new Finoola yesterday.

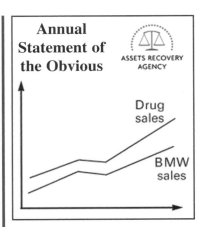

Annual Statement of the Obvious

ASSETS RECOVERY AGENCY

Drug sales

BMW sales

POLICE SERVICE of NORTHERN IRELAND
A Service to be Proud of

ANNUAL REPORT 2003

Solving crimes	**0%**
Catching criminals	**0%**
Shutting down nightclubs for serving after hours	**100%**

The PSNI
**Half Catholic
Half Protestant
Half arsed**

JOHN WHITE FINDS GOD

by our religious affairs correspondent, Helen Brimstone

JOHN WHITE has found God. Mr White discovered the supreme Creator of all things while searching for some of his other friends under a rock.

'I asked God to perform a miracle,' Mr White told reporters yesterday, 'and he immediately turned a box of prison handicrafts into a £200,000 house outside Carrickfergus. Praise Him.'

The Portadown News

15TH JULY 2003 www.PortadownNews.com

RACIST ATTACK HORROR

by our Craigavon correspondent, Barry Dogshit

Craigavon loyalist Billy Shootspatrick has ordered his girlfriend Shelley-Anne McAvoy (14) to leave the country, after a fake tan went horribly wrong.

'I told her to get a nice orange colour for the twelfth,' Mr Shootspatrick told our reporter yesterday, 'but she came home as black as the ace of spades. Obviously I had no choice but to hand her an anonymous death threat then set fire to the living room.'

'It's a pity Shelley-Anne wasn't one of them there Muslimists,' added Mr Shootspatrick. 'Then I could just have put a bag over her head.'

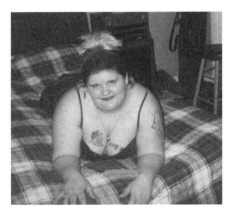

CRAP CRISIS CONTINUES

by our republican correspondent, Anne Phoblacht

REAL IRA inmates at Maghaberry say their dirty protest will 'run and run'.

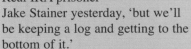

'We're being denied our human rights,' claimed Real IRA prisoner Jake Stainer yesterday, 'but we'll be keeping a log and getting to the bottom of it.'

The Prison Service has described the allegations as 'a smear campaign'.

THE BONFIRE CODE

- Use unleaded petrol
- Point gas cylinders upwards
- Move children indoors
- Move children with doors
- Think 'I recognise that sofa'

Confusing republicans

A cut-out-and-keep guide

Language activist

Eco-tourists

Woman

Til death do they part?

by our health correspondent, Florence Crippen

PEOPLE will die from terminal boredom if the Hospice crisis is not resolved soon, an independent review has warned.

'The two factions have been fighting over nothing for years,' says the report. 'Obviously, the Northern Ireland public finds this completely inexplicable.'

Personal hygiene latest:
Freak showers in Newry

See page 42

Sean declared kosher

by our West Belfast correspondent, Gerry Andersonstown

Phobaile Baile Feirst fir Seán Ó Muireagáin is finally saoirse. 'Ceud mille sháloms!' he said yesterlá, 'ich bin ein bin-lid.'

Méanwhilé Isráéli 'Mossád' sécurocráts agus Andérsonstown Nuacht ééjits both 'blámé thé Brits' Lá-Lá-Lá usual story, but an Sinn Féin spokésfir said, 'No pictures. God bless Américá!'

© *Hurriedly translated without permission from the Belfast Telegraph, as usual*

Sinn Féin Anti-Racism Policy

SINN FÉIN

Any colour you like

As long as it's green

BBC
Northern Ireland

'The Twelfth'

12:00	Dignified parades
13:00	Short sermons
17:00	Inflammatory speeches
17:01	Serious drinking
17:02	Sporadic violence
18:00	Sustained violence
19:30	Inter-band brawling
22:00	Show of strength
23:00	UDA feuding (may over-run)
23:57	Underage sex
23:59	National Anthem
24:00	CLOSEDOWN (of entire country)

Sinn Fein T-shirts

available online from:

www.hypocrisy.co.uk

Anger at dumping plan

by our republican correspondent, Anne Phoblacht

Real IRA inmates at Maghaberry have denied claims that their planned hunger strike will mean an end to their ongoing dirty protest.

'Food or no food,' said spokesman Rory O'Splitter yesterday, 'we'll still be full of crap until the day we die.'

Spanish blast latest:

Mayor caught in bomb not planted by previous mayor
See page 42

NEWSLETTER SOLD

by our business correspondent, Reg Empty

A leading local businessman is understood to have bought the Newsletter.

Mr Roy Bailout acquired the newspaper yesterday morning for a sum believed to be in the region of 50p.

VICTIMS MYSTIFIED BY UNPROVOKED SECTARIAN ATTACKS

See page

Belfast Telegraph in Portadown News shock

By Claire Regan and Ashleigh Wallace

A PLUCKY pensioner whose roof was destroyed by a massive lightning strike discharged herself

(Front page lead story, Wednesday's Telly)

Fancy a REAL holiday?

Camping in Tipperary

Ages 10 and up
Warning: outdoor pursuits may end up inside.

Dissident Republican Amoebas

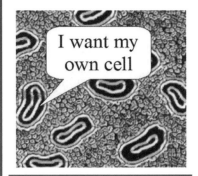

STORM THE BARRICADES

by our weather correspondent, John Humid

The air remained tense in Belfast today after rival clouds clashed overnight. Both sides put up a front and the atmosphere soon became highly charged.

'As usual my officers were there to provide a positive force on the ground,' explained PSNI Chief Constable Gareth Millwall, 'but once again I must appeal to all residents to stop conducting themselves.'

Chief Constable in 'political remarks' shock

Relief of Derry

by our North West correspondent, Dermont Londondermont

This year's Maiden City Festival has passed off without incident.

'Parity of esteem for our shared culture is the way forward for both communities,' an Apprentice Boys spokesman told our reporter yesterday.

'Now let's see the fenians get out of that one.'

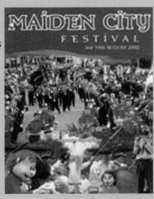

THANKS A MILLION!

A moving tribute to the generosity of the Northern Ireland Office

NI Events Company	£1.2m
Ulster-Scots Agency	£4.1m
Arts Council	£13m
Youth Community Relations	£25.5m
Welfare to Work	£44.6m
Omagh Legal Fund*	£0.8m

(*and only a five-year wait)

Figures from 2003/2004 Executive Budget

Drumcree

www.PortadownNews.com

"WE'RE BLACK", SAY ORANGEMEN

by our race relations correspondent, Mohammed Mpofu

Orange Order Grand Wizard Robert Saulters raised eyebrows at last week's Drumcree standoff by claiming that Orangemen are black.

"We are the victims of cultural apartheid," said Mr Saulters, "so Sinn Fein needn't compare us to the Afrikaaners – we're the nig-nogs in this situation."

"No, we're black," say residents

However Garvaghy Road Residents Committee Chairperson Brendan McKenna immediately hit back. "The Orange Order is marching through our neighbourhood just like the Klu Klux Klan, so actually *we're* the jungle bunnies in Portadown."

"Arseholes," say RUC

Now local RUC constable Bill Mason has stepped into the argument. "If that's what they think," he said yesterday, "I'd like to know why they both keep calling me a 'Black Bastard'."

RUN! HIDE! IT'S THE. . .
ATTACK OF THE ORANGEMEN

PERAMBULATE!
PERAMBULATE!

doktormoog@hotmail.com

FOR SALE

Announcements
PORTADOWN JULY CLOSING DOWN SALE

Everyone must go (on holiday)

Drumcree: look who's talking

by our Drumcree correspondent, Will March

Archbishop Robin Eames ➡ **God**

I know talking to God is pointless, but it's still better than talking to the Reverend Pickering.

Harold Gracey ➡ **The Caravan Club**

In my experience the Hillmaster 2000 is totally unsuitable for anyone planning a longer-than-usual holiday.

Brendan McKenna ➡ **The media**

' . . so then Gerry said, "Connect the brown wire to the chassis and the green wire to the alternator . . ."

Councillor David Jones ➡ **Himself**

I'm not talking to you.

EXCLUSIVE! Drumcree VIII Battle Map

Now you can follow the most important geopolitical event of the year from the comfort of your living room, with the **Portadown News Drumcree Battle Map**.

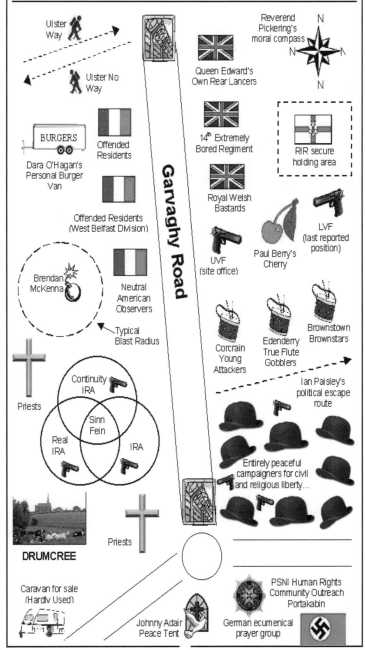

Ulster Way

Ulster No Way

Reverend Pickering's moral compass

Queen Edward's Own Rear Lancers

14th Extremely Bored Regiment

RIR secure holding area

BURGERS

Dara O'Hagan's Personal Burger Van

Offended Residents

Royal Welsh Bastards

Offended Residents (West Belfast Division)

Garvaghy Road

Brendan McKenna

Neutral American Observers

UVF (site office)

Paul Berry's Cherry

LVF (last reported position)

Typical Blast Radius

Corcrain Young Attackers

Edenderry True Flute Gobblers

Brownstown Brownstars

Priests

Continuity IRA

Sinn Fein

Real IRA

IRA

Ian Paisley's political escape route

Entirely peaceful campaigners for civil and religious liberty...

DRUMCREE

Priests

Caravan for sale (Hardly Used)

Johnny Adair Peace Tent

German ecumenical prayer group

PSNI Human Rights Community Outreach Portakabin

The Portadown News

12TH AUGUST 2003   www.PortadownNews.com

IS THIS WHAT YOU WANT?

This is what our beauty spots will look like unless we stop complaining about windmills and start tackling our mates in the building trade.

STOP OUR MADNESS, WRITE TO:

The Bribery Officer, Causeway Borough Council, Development House, Ballyraine

---

CAR KIDNAP CRISIS

by our loyalist correspondent, Billy Shootspatrick

The Real IRA has admitted responsibility for this week's kidnap attempt on Billy Hutchinson, who was out jogging when four men tried to abduct him.

'We were after a senior UVF commander,' explained a RIRA spokesman yesterday, 'but this guy was obviously just a runner.'

EXAM QUESTION

by our education correspondent, Una O'Level

RADIATION FROM SELLAFIELD may have caused this year's record-breaking A-level results, claim a local scientist.

'The Government insists that A-levels aren't getting easier,' explained Dr Bunsen Burns yesterday, 'so the intelligence of the average 18-year-old must have doubled in the past ten years. Unchecked, this mutation could lead to a race of telepathic superbeings sworn to enslave the rest of humanity. Those who got four A-grades must be dissected immediately.'

A rabbit yesterday.

Education officials have rejected the claims. 'Dissection is no longer taught at A-Level,' said a spokesman. 'Instead, students write a short essay on how it feels to be a rabbit.'

Small big cat crisis

by our tourism correspondent, Johnny Foreigner

TOURISTS have nothing to fear from the puma which escaped last week on the North Coast, say police.

'Cats are very clean animals,' explained PSNI officer Bill Mason yesterday, 'so it won't be going anywhere near Portrush.'

Think of the Children International

Summer Holiday Appeal

Every year we bring a group of American children to Northern Ireland to enjoy a holiday away from their troubled country. Children like little Brad Cheeseburger (15 stone) have known nothing but terrorism and

war since the coup three years ago. Electricity is now a luxury, human rights have been suppressed and public health care is illegal. PLEASE GIVE GENEROUSLY. THESE KIDS HAVE SUFFERED ENOUGH.

SHOOT-TO-KILL ALLEGATION

by our republican correspondent, Anne Phoblacht

REPUBLICANS have accused the police of operating a 'feline shoot-to-kill' policy.

'We'll be taking this all the way to Brussels,' warned a spokesman for the Cat Finucane Centre yesterday.

Declaration of a Bill of Rights

We hold these truths to be self-evident, that all men (and women) are created equal (as defined by the Equality Commission), that they are endowed by Brice Dickson with certain unalienable rights, that among these are life, liberty and the pursuit of their legitimate constitutional aspiration within an agreed legal framework –

That to secure these rights, Quangos are instituted among men (and women) deriving their just powers from the consent of the government . . .

> . . . and so forth for verily another 400 pages

POLICE OPEN DISCLOSURE

by our security correspondent, Roger Base

NEW DISCLOSURE RULES will require police officers to declare their membership of the PSNI.

'Look mate, I'm in the force myself,' officer Bill Mason informed colleagues at a speed-trap last night, adding, 'of course this is my bloody vehicle.'

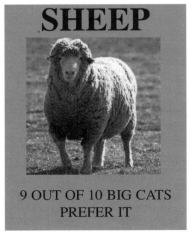

ULSTER'S BIG CAT CRISIS

by our big cat correspondent, John Cougar

Police have vowed to 'Bring the cat in', despite failing to capture any of the animals terrorising Ulster.

'Cubs have been scouted, leopards have been spotted and ocelots have been seen a lot,' admitted PSNI Officer Bill Mason yesterday, speaking by radio from his 2.2 litre Jaguar. 'However I want the public to know that we're not lion down on the job.'

PORTADOWN
Golf Course

Now open to members of the Travelling Community*
*by court order

 changing rooms

This week the team travel to Bolton, where they help Gina and friends transform their council houses on a budget of just £50,000 per week (minus dealer's cut).

Rangers fans appeal
by our crime correspondent, Rob Berry

POLICE have asked Rangers fans to help them find UDA Godfather John Gregg's killers.

'This was a lethal and well co-ordinated attack,' officer Bill Mason told reporters yesterday, 'so at least we can rule out Tore Andre Flo.'

Enniskillen latest:
Collapsing flats claim 'without foundation'
See page 42

ALL COKED UP
by our American correspondent, Brad Cheeseburger

The Coca-Cola Company has defended its $5,000 donation to Sinn Fein.

'Coca Cola and Sinn Fein share the same goals,' explained a spokesman, 'such as togetherness, refreshment and total world domination.'

'I don't know anything about Coke,' Sinn Fein Councillor Kerry Jelly told our reporter yesterday, 'but I can get you three pills for a tenner.'

ANOTHER ISRAEL STORY

by our Jerusalem correspondent, Olive Mount

Another Palestinian has committed suicide after watching a report by BBC Middle East correspondent, Orla Guerin.

'Another day, another body, another depressing cliché lent false weight by the heavy, ever-sinking tones of my glum half-Dublin accent,' said Ms Guerin yesterday.

Irish Republic latest:
Fat people face heavy tax
See page 57

Ulster GAA latest:
All-British All-Ireland?
See page 57

RESTORATION
Which ruin will you vote to preserve?

Trimble Towers
Cold, remote lodge with split-level foundation. Requires considerable underpinning.

Durkan's Mill
Impressive but largely empty structure in prime political location. Suitable for conversion.

Shinnerfield Hall
Expensive wartime folly with elaborate plaster façade. Fairly solid rear but front keeps slipping.

Ervine's Puppy Farm
Rambling, isolated property with outside WC. Prone to rot.

Tragic remains washed up after 30 years

"We should probably 'disappear' for a few days"

"I know this great beach . . ."

Hunt for the Disappeared continues

Thinking of moving?

Fully licensed, apparently

DIG FOR VICTORY

BBC RADIO BLUSTER

Backtalk's David Dunluce talks to Ballymena DUP Councillor Shootspatrick (followed by Sectarian Thought for the Day)

Dunluce: Is bigotry a problem in Ballymena?

Shootspatrick: No – you're just biased against us.

Dunluce: What makes you think we're biased?

Shootspatrick: Because you're all a bunch of dirty fenians!

Utterly useless team loses twelve times in a row

ALL-ULSTER UNIONIST FINAL

by our unionist correspondent, Will March

 V

UUP final fever has gripped Northern Ireland this week as both sides of Reg Empey gear up for the Leadership Cup.

'It's not often you see two sides of Reg Empey in the final,' one UUP fan told our reporter yesterday. 'It'll be hard to get a seat, especially in East Belfast.'

Panther latest:

Big cat blamed for ram raid

See page 57

BURIED TREASURE
by our crime correspondent, Rob Berry

THE ASSETS RECOVERY AGENCY has seized property worth £1.5m belonging to deceased Red Hand Commando leader Jim Johnston.

'This is a major step towards curtailing Mr Johnston's criminal activities,' said a spokesman yesterday. 'We're making life increasingly difficult for dead loyalists.'

*I*RVINE CRITIC 'NOT JEALOUS'
by our sarcasm correspondent, I. Wright

Local man Gareth Spoiler is 'definitely not jealous' of former F1 driver Eddie Irvine.

'My burning hatred of Eddie Irvine, who I have never met, is entirely rational,' Mr Spoiler told our reporter last night, before driving his fat girlfriend home in a 1.1-litre Renault Clio.

Glorious football victory!
by our Armenian correspondent, Yerman in Yerevan

GOAL ARMENIA!
Northern Ireland zog in UEFA gulag vodka George Best 'turning in his grave'.

Commissar Sammy McIlvitch Pravda, 'Frankly Ivan, we need a f*cking revolution.'

Assembly latest: Democracy replaced by Thursday repeat of 'Hearts & Minds'

See page 57

Michael Stone in appearance fee shock

Sure I'll do weddings . . . but I prefer funerals

Have Your Say!
Is the IRA involved in threatening Catholic Policing Board members?

Andy Townnews, West Belfast
'Well, Martin McGuinness says no, and it's not like he'd look right into a camera and lie his head off, now, is it?'

Ian Gough-Barracks, Armagh
'I really have no idea, but a dark unacknowledged part of me sincerely hopes so.'

Alice Sprucefield, Holywood
'It's terrible, it really is. They'd never have let Catholics on the Policing Board in my day.'

Situations Vacant

Portadown News
JobSeeker

Urgently required:

Chicken Wanker

Salary – £4.20 per litre
Tweezers provided

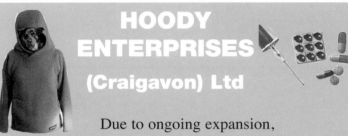

HOODY ENTERPRISES (Craigavon) Ltd

Due to ongoing expansion,

we wish to employ a

Drug Dealer

This is an excellent opportunity for a young self-starter,

with a view to future self-employment.

Somebody else's phone and car essential.

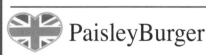 PaisleyBurger

Portadown's leading DUP-owned
meat processor

Following legal action,
we have been advised to hire a

Token Catholic

*This position is permanent –
although we don't expect you to last any
longer than the others did.*

Police Service of Northern Ireland
www.parapolice.uk   0044 (0) 26 90550222

Due to a recent suicide,
we have a vacancy for:

Chief Constable

The successful candidate will prevent crime
through a policy of *human rights facilitation*.

The successful candidate will then take the
blame when it all goes horribly wrong.

Apply in crayon to Nuala O'Loan

Situations Vacant

Portadown Youth Centre
wishes to hire a

Riot Co-ordinator

Minimum requirements

- 2 years' experience organising street disturbances
- GCSE Media Studies
- NVQ Level 3 'Community Exploitation'

We are an equal-opportunity employer

Portadown 'Town of Culture'

Quango Co-ordinator

The successful applicant will:

- Get paid loads of money
- Go to lots of parties
- Be in all the papers
- Quit at the very last minute
- Then call everyone else cynical ...

Portadown News
JobSeeker

Belfast City Council

Council Employee
£30K pa just for turning up

Northern Ireland Assembly

Assembly Member
£30K pa for <u>not</u> turning up

SOCIAL SECURITY AGENCY NORTHERN IRELAND

Every other job in Northern Ireland
£4.50 an hour for the rest of your life

May Pork

IT'S NEARLY MEAT!

Due to a recent television programme, we have vacancies for Illegal Immigrants

(please apply through your local mafia)

The Portadown News

23RD SEPTEMBER 2003   www.PortadownNews.com

LOYALISTS PICKET BIRTHS

by our loyalist correspondent, Billy Shootspatrick

LOYALISTS have picketed Portadown Maternity Hospital demanding an end to caesarean sections. 'Caesar was Roman,' one protestor told our reporter yesterday, 'and now they've gone and set up a whole Roman section.'

Asked if he felt the situation was grave, a UDA spokesman said, 'No – that was last weekend.'

None shall de-foetus

Belfast's own goal

by our business correspondent, Reg Empty

The Tourist Board has welcomed news that Crumlin Road prison is to be turned into a visitor attraction.

'This will be just like Alcatraz in San Francisco,' explained a Tourist Board spokesman yesterday, 'except that in Belfast we put the gays in jail and the gangsters in the nightclubs.'

Up the Crum yesterday

Not a bullet . . .

by our republican correspondent, Anne Phoblacht

The Real IRA has admitted that sending bullets to Policing Board members is technically an act of decommissioning.

'From now on we'll keep our bullets and just say we've sent them,' said Real IRA spokesman Rory O'Splitter yesterday.

However, the Northern Ireland Office has claimed that this is technically decommissioning as well.

. . . or an ounce of sense

Blair opens trees

by our security correspondent, Roger Base

Tony Blair has opened the new security forces memorial tree garden, conveniently located in England to avoid embarrassment.

'Trees are the perfect memorial to the security forces,' Mr Blair told weeping mourners. 'They have bark but no bite, many special branches, and end up being treated like planks. Now please leave.'

Portadown News Sports Update

George Best v Death

57-0 with extra time

Alex Higgins v Life

No score draw

ANOTHER DAY IN PARADISE

by our cynical correspondent, Paddy O'Really

An elderly woman has been eaten by a tiger after a teenage rapist knocked her unconscious during a riot in a graveyard. An ambulance despatched to the scene collided with a joyrider after an overweight child threw a pipe bomb through the windscreen. The driver was charged with child abuse and received a death threat for talking to the police. His house was later petrol bombed, then illegally demolished by a property developer.

The tiger remains at large.

Labour welcomes Northern Ireland members

Christ, here come the paddies

ULSTER-SCOTS PERVERT IN TERRIBLE MISUNDERSTANDING SHOCK

I said 'Burns Night' not 'Bairns Night'

Team not guilty

by our sports correspondent, Ed Balls

No Northern Ireland players are involved in the gang-rape scandal rocking the world of football, the Portadown News can exclusively reveal.

'None of our guys has scored in years,' said a source yesterday.

UUP IN ELECTION CALL

by our unionist correspondent, Will March

The Ulster Unionist Party has called for Assembly elections to be held 'as soon as possible'.

'I see no reason why elections shouldn't be held today,' said a UUP spokesman this morning. 'Especially in Armagh and Tyrone, between the hours of 2 o'clock and 4 o'clock.'

'Dope & Mystery'

**by Gerry Adams
An exclusive extract from the long-awaited sequel to 'Before the Brawn'**

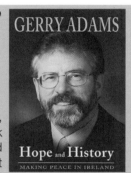

'We negotiated long into the night, despite the fact that nobody would talk to us – except once, when I bumped into David Trimble in the toilet. "We must stop meeting like this," I said, because I am terribly witty. "You must stop killing people," Mr Trimble barked back angrily. Honestly, there's just no talking to that man.

Did I mention that I love trees?'

School bomb latest:
UDA launches 'weapons of class destruction'

See page 57

FAT-CATS OF THE LAND

by our agriculture correspondent, Culchie McMucker

The Department of Agriculture has launched an investigation into farmers who have stolen money through the so-called 'paper acres' scam.

Meanwhile, farmers have launched an investigation into the Department of Agriculture for stealing money through the so-called 'acres of paper' scam.

TELE-TABBY TERROR!

by our big cat correspondent, Oscar Lyons

This is the first shocking picture of the big cat currently terrorising the Belfast Telegraph. An expert who examined our exclusive photo this morning confirmed that the animal is either '200 feet tall' or 'very close to the camera indeed'.

'You are the most irresponsible and parochial journalist I have ever met,' PSNI officer Bill Mason told our reporter yesterday. However, Officer Mason refused to deny that lions will attack children who poke them with sticks.

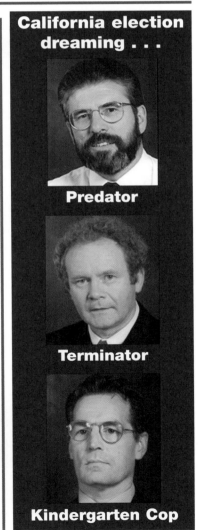

California election dreaming . . .

Predator

Terminator

Kindergarten Cop

BLOODY Sunday INQUIRY

Day 1,281

Lord Saville:	So who was shooting at you?
Soldier 46:	One of the natives, definitely.
Volunteer 23:	I heard it was Martin.
Lawyer 631:	Objection! My client was in church at the time.
Lord Saville:	Don't you mean mass?
Soldier 46:	No, he got me in the leg.
Clerk 87:	Ha! That's a cracker.
Lord Saville:	Let's adjourn for £300 million.

DON'T BANK ON IT

by our crime correspondent, Rob Berry

This is dramatic footage of the bank employees who shocked Northern Ireland by trying to stop money being thrown away.

'We need to ask ourselves where we're heading when people can't even be trusted to waste millions of pounds,' PSNI officer Bill Mason told our reporter yesterday.

However, police do not believe that the crime was sectarian, as the notes involved were of all denominations.

Our Wee Jeffrey

2003   www.PortadownNews.com

Portadown News
JobSeeker

Ulster Unionist Party

Wanted: Candidate for
LAGAN VALLEY

The successful applicant must demonstrate a full understanding that David Trimble is in charge.

Portadown News
JobSeeker

DEMOCRATIC UNIONISTS

Wanted: Candidate for
LAGAN VALLEY

The successful applicant must demonstrate a full understanding that Peter Robinson is in charge.

NUMBERS UP

UUC delegates opposed to power sharing
46%

Catholic population of Northern Ireland
46%

Steven Queen
PORTADOWN'S FAVOURITE UNIONIST COLUMNIST

'It's the question every father dreads: "So daddy, what did you do during the 10th Ulster Unionist Council crisis meeting?"

'How well I remember the ill-fated charge of the Lisburn Brigade, riding once more into the Lagan Valley of Death . . .'

(and so on)

A Portadown News In-Depth Report:
Who's behind Jeffrey?

DAVID SIDEBURN (51)	DARLENE FESTER (56)	REV. MARTYN LUTHER (104)
Joined Vanguard as a van guard. Lives in London, Antrim and denial. Sees himself as the next Jeffrey Donaldson, preferably within the year.	Became an Ulster Unionist because, 'There's nothing else to do in Fermanagh.' Described by the Woman's Coalition as 'The wrong sort of woman'.	Affectionately known as 'Daisy' by the late Sir Edward Carson, Luther says his political beliefs stem from 'an intense religious ~~hatred~~ faith'.

Half-life of the party

by our unionist correspondent Will March

DUBLIN has called on the British Government to close the controversial Unionist Reprocessing Party.

'Dangerous elements have been exposed and there is a serious risk of fall-out,' warned an Irish government official yesterday. 'Their core values are all over the place. Something needs to be done before there's a complete meltdown.'

The Unionist Reprocessing Party said it had no reaction.

Selloutfield yesterday

SHAM FIGHT SHAMBLES

by our unionist correspondent, Will March

In a tradition as old as Northern Ireland itself, David Trimble will once again battle against Jeffrey Donaldson at today's annual Scarva Sham Fight.

'David will win for the 313th time but of course Jeffrey will be back next year to do it all over again,' said a unionist spokesman yesterday, before bursting into tears.

Unionist vote scandal

by our unionist correspondent, Will March

A leading member of the Ulster Unionist Party has been accused of electoral misrepresentation.

Mr Jeffrey Donaldson (5'2") is believed to have made repeated claims that a 46% vote constituted 'the majority of unionists'. Several other men are also helping nobody with their enquiries.

Donaldson and Burnside agree on way forward

You're next

Islamic invasion terror!

by our religious affairs correspondent, Helen Brimstone

Christians are fleeing for their lives this weekend as the Islamic hordes pour relentlessly into Portadown, threatening to slaughter us all.

'For the love of God, why didn't we listen to Ulster Unionist Councillor Fred Crowe?' exclaimed popular Brownstown girl Shelley-Anne McAvoy as she was expertly dismembered by an Arabian scimitar. 'If only we hadn't granted planning permission for that Mosque!' screamed well-known Killicomaine pensioner Harold Mothball as he was horribly mauled by a rabid camel.

Although the PSNI have described both incidents as 'not sectarian', it seems that Portadown's hard-won reputation for religious tolerance has been seriously tarnished.

Craigavon Councillor Fred Crowe

Muslims cause mayhem

by our unionist correspondent, Will March

DUP Deputy Mayor David Simpson has issued a statement condemning UUP Councillor Fred Crowe's racist remarks on Monday's BBC Newsline.

'Does this mean that the DUP is now less bigoted than the UUP?' one confused local resident asked our reporter yesterday. 'These Muslims are turning Northern Ireland society upside-down.'

Mosque plan unveiled

by our mosque correspondent, Minny Rette

Plans for the new Portadown Mosque were unveiled in the town hall yesterday.

Stop Press: We have just been informed that the new Portadown Mosque plans must remain veiled at all times.

INMATES TO BE SEGREGATED

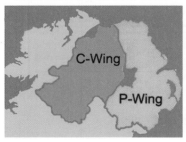

C-Wing

P-Wing

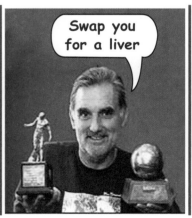

Swap you for a liver

Cranes 'a lasting symbol of Belfast'

PROTESTANT

CATHOLIC

'Misunderstanding' claim

by our religious affairs correspondent, Helen Brimstone

Local resident Mr Ali Akhbar Yassirarafat believes he may be responsible for Councillor Fred Crowe's claim that 'Muslims want to kill Christians'.

'I was at a council planning meeting earlier this week,' Mr Yassirarafat told our reporter yesterday, 'and when the meeting ended I said "Let's shoot the crow". My remarks may have been misunderstood. Sorry about that now.'

'Sorry about that now'

Timetable of tragedy

8:17	Tony Blair announces elections to an assembly that doesn't exist.
10:23	Gerry Adams makes statement on behalf of an organisation that he doesn't belong to.
15:41	General de Chastelain confirms that he doesn't have permission to confirm anything.
17:01	David Trimble says he doesn't believe a word of it.
17:02	Jeffrey Donaldson doesn't believe his luck.
19:16	Bertie Ahern says he doesn't know what went wrong, so he doesn't.
00:00	Everybody else says, 'Thank God this stuff doesn't really matter.'

Bus stop stopped

by our public transport correspondent, Dee Railment

Bus drivers have threatened to cause traffic chaos this week by not striking.

'We're going to drive very slowly down every main route into the city, stopping every fifty yards and not letting anybody past,' one angry driver warned our reporter yesterday.

A Translink spokesman said all services should be running normally.

The Portadown News

28TH OCTOBER 2003   www.PortadownNews.com

Blame the Canadian

by our security correspondent, Roger Base

SECURITY CHIEFS are furious after Tony Blair accidentally revealed that Britain monitors all IRA arms dumps around the clock. Mr Blair made the gaff after unionists rejected a decommissioning statement by General John de Chastelain.

'If only you knew what I knew,' said the Prime Minister. 'If only I knew how you knew,' responded General de Chastelain. 'How do you know if he knows you don't know?' asked Ian Paisley. 'Look, there's Concorde!' said Mr Blair before running from the room.

It's all his fault

Downing Street is blaming General de Chastelain for the crisis. 'We will distract the media by blaming a weapons inspector for our mistake,' warned a spin doctor yesterday. 'Let's just hope this one doesn't kill himself.'

Leaders 'still agree on fundamentals'

Gotcha!

JUST THE MAN

by our religious affairs correspondent, Helen Brimstone

Armagh Primate Robin Eames has been chosen to mediate in the 'gay bishops' row.

'This debate has a lot in common with the Northern Ireland peace process,' explained a church spokesman yesterday. 'We also need to find a bottom line both sides can agree on.'

Not to be sniffed at

by our loyalist correspondent, Billy Shootspatrick

Police sources have expressed their amazement at the huge LVF drugs haul seized in Portadown this week.

'First they try selling ecstasy in a town with no nightclubs, then they try selling cocaine in a town with no middle class,' PSNI Officer Bill Mason told our reporter yesterday. 'Why don't they just smuggle tobacco like everyone else?'

Was tower the target?

by our security correspondent, Roger Base

The Al-Qaeda suspect arrested in Newtownards was planning to fly a plane into Scrabo Tower, the Portadown News can sensationally speculate.

The 26-year-old Algerian may have considered taking flying lessons at Newtownards Airport, although they're terribly expensive you know, and there's a much better bar at the yacht club.

'Today could well have been our 9/11,' claimed PSNI officer Bill Mason this morning, 'because unlike the Americans we write down the day first, then the month. Otherwise it would be our 11/9.'

MAKE IT GO AWAY

by our North West correspondent, Dermont Londondermont

THIRTEEN innocent civilians have died laughing after Martin McGuinness opened fire on the Bloody Sunday Inquiry.

'It was chaos,' a witness told our reporter yesterday. 'One minute everything was perfectly civil right, then suddenly people were falling over completely helpless . . .'
(continued until the money runs out)

North West latest:
Londonderry demands shorter name, longer runway

Four steps to decommissioning

1. Hidden deal
2. Invisible movement
3. Opaque statement
4. Transparent disaster

Today's burgled pensioner is:

Plucky Alice Mothball, 93, beaten senseless, savings stolen, community outraged, police sickened, what's the world coming to? etc. etc.

Customer Notice

TO SERVE YOU BETTER, THE PHONE BOOK WILL NO LONGER BE PUBLISHED
To complain, please call BT Directory Enquiries (£1/min) and ask for the Complaints Hotline

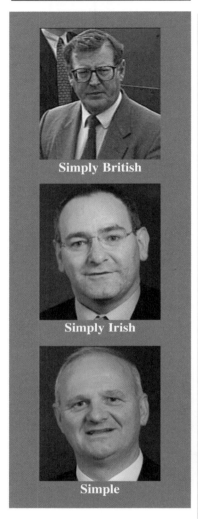

Simply British

Simply Irish

Simple

WHERE EAGLES DAREN'T

by our European correspondent, Ann Twerpe

Details have been released of 'Plan Kathleen', the joint Nazi-IRA wartime invasion plan. German special forces would have landed at Nutts Corner Airfield and erected an enormous headquarters building (or 'Lidl') to prepare for a summer invasion of the North Coast.

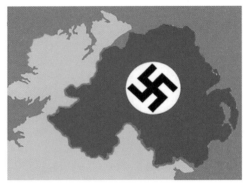

Ourselves, Ein Volk, Alone

Internment camps would have been set up in Belfast and Sinn Fein placed in charge of a fascist political system.

'Few historians take "Plan Kathleen" that seriously,' one expert told our reporter yesterday. 'There was obviously no chance of any of this stuff actually happening.'

BELFAST

BALLYMENA

Protestant tries withdrawal method

I can go another three weeks!

Catriona Ruane in parachute regiment shock

SMALL RISE IN UNEMPLOYMENT PREDICTED

Too much lead in local water, politics

In Depth

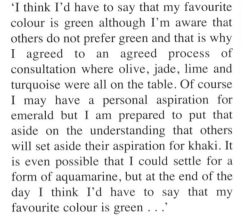
VOTE **2003** NORTHERN IRELAND

This week we ask SDLP Leader Mark Durkan: What's your favourite colour?

'I think I'd have to say that my favourite colour is green although I'm aware that others do not prefer green and that is why I agreed to an agreed process of consultation where olive, jade, lime and turquoise were all on the table. Of course I may have a personal aspiration for emerald but I am prepared to put that aside on the understanding that others will set aside their aspiration for khaki. It is even possible that I could settle for a form of aquamarine, but at the end of the day I think I'd have to say that my favourite colour is green . . .'

(continued for as long as you can bear it)

DUP BATTLE-BUS TIMETABLE

19:50	Ballymena
19:74	Sunningdale (request stop)
19:86	Clontibret (via Garda station)
19:98	Hillsborough (Not Good Friday)
20:03	UUP head office
20:04	Stormont (all change)

Unionist crime-wave latest:
Elderly man attacked at bus stop

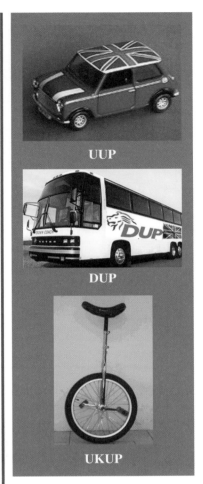

UUP

DUP

UKUP

TERRORIST MANUAL 'DIFFICULT TO TRANSLATE'

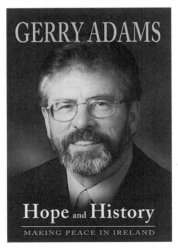

Exclusive election poll

How will you vote?

96%	With a pencil
Yes	After 'Eastenders'
2	Twice

Are 3-D graphs confusing?

Not sure   Maybe

Who ate all the pie charts?

DAVID TRIMBLE 100%

Do you understand proportional representation?

1	2	3	4	5	6
No	No	No	No	No	No
Yes	Yes	Yes	Yes	Yes	Yes

Have you roached your polling card?

Yes   No

Is opinion divided?

Yes	No
No	Yes

I would rather die . . . than deviate from my prepared answer

UlsterUnionists

The future, not the prat

Campaign Notebook
Our light-hearted election diary

■ **DUP CANDIDATE** Billy Homer wants David Trimble to enjoy some Portadown hospitality. 'I'll be happy to shake his hand,' says Billy, 'then the mob I've arranged can start kicking him to death.'

■ Few politicians dread going out to canvas as much as North Belfast independent Desmond Cordner. That's because there's a UDA police informer hanging around trying to shoot him!

■ Tyrone SDLP candidate Mary Castle is having a good laugh at the Real IRA team that's promised to kill her. 'Last night they painted "Die Fenian Bitch" on the car', she tells me with a smile between tranquillisers.

■ 'Aren't all these death threats against people just terrible?' I ask Sinn Fein's Laughlin McMitchell. 'No,' he says. You can always count on a Derry man for a straight answer!

BELFAST

LONDONDERRY

Constituency Profile:
Upper Down

The Upper Down constituency comprises those areas of County Down more than 1,000 feet above sea level, plus a short section of the sea-bed 12 miles west of Rathlin Island.

This has created an unusual situation in the village of Dromore, where the top floors of many houses are in Upper Down while their ground floors are in Lower Down. As a result some Protestant residents feel they have been denied a vote, as they are more likely to live in bungalows . . .

. . . and so on

1998 Results	
Good Prods	20%
Evil Prods	20%
Good Taigs	20%
Evil Taigs	20%
Nutters	20%

LISBURN
A city* for everyone**

*Not actual size
**Except Catholics

WC goes down the pan
by our women's correspondent, A. Baird

There were tears and big hugs across North Down last night as the Women's Coalition was consigned to history.

'It is time for us to respect the wishes of the public and leave the cut and thrust of democratic politics behind us,' party spokesman Jane Williams told our reporter this morning. Ms Williams will now take up a £90,000-a-year position at the newly-established Women's Commission.

Power cut hits traffic lights

VOTERS CHOOSE EVIL
by our religion correspondent, Helen Brimstone

The forces of darkness are celebrating a historic victory in this week's assembly elections.

'I listened to both sides but in the end I felt that evil would best represent my community,' said one voter yesterday. 'The forces of good have had their chance,' said another. 'It's time to give evil a go.'

Despite this set-back for the peace process, the Northern Ireland Office is still confident that it can bridge the yawning chasm of Hades. 'Eventually evil will recognise that good must always triumph in the end,' explained an NIO spokesman. 'Besides we already have quite a lot of experience of working with evil, especially at the local council level.'

The Portadown News

www.PortadownNews.com

Paisley in secret Dublin talks

If you think you've got a heroin problem, you should see Ballymena

---

Northern Ireland Electricity –
The men behind the wire

CUSTOMER NOTICE

We wish to apologise for the current situation, which is due to an unexpected surge of resistance.

Normal service is now resumed

US envoy leaves Northern Ireland

I'm sending you to Iraq

Thank Christ

BBC RADIO BLUSTER

Seamus Austin struggles to fill 326 hours of airtime while old ladies count ballots in a leisure centre. Followed by Sectarian Thought for the Day.

Seamus – Still no results from Upper Down. Judith Collins, what do you make of that?

Judith – Obviously the Brits have told the old ladies to count slowly to delay the inevitable reunification of Ireland.

Seamus – Steven Queen, there are loads of old ladies in the UUP. Couldn't they help out here?

Steven – I'll have to correct you there, Seamus. What we have in the Ulster Unionist Party is a load of old women . . .

. . . and so on

Mediation Northern Ireland
Creative approaches to better relations

After 659 attacks on his home, local resident George Trevor takes PSNI advice and enters into mediation with the UDA.

George – Please, please, please leave my family alone.

UDA – Whaddya mean like? It wasn't us like. Are you startin? We'll put yer f***ing windas in!

George – There isn't a single window left in the house.

UDA – Are you trying to be smart like? Are you? Don't you try being smart with us you f***ing fenian-lover, we'll kill you so we well, you're f***ing dead so you are...

...continued until somebody calls the ombudsman and forces the police to do their f*ing job**

BACK TO THE DARK AGES

by our economics correspondent, Reg Empty

THE NORTHERN IRELAND OFFICE has announced that it organised this week's power cuts to demonstrate what life in the 17th century really feels like. The Portadown News understands that plans to switch the water off and let the roads fall apart are also at an advanced stage.

"If you're not going forward then you're going back," said an NIO official yesterday. "Slap it up you."

The DUP has criticised the move. "The government needs to understand that just because we've said we don't want power, that doesn't mean we aren't still planning to use it," explained a party spokesman.

DON'T SHOP AND DRIVE

by our security correspondent, Roger Base

The PSNI has launched its annual 'Don't Shop and Drive' campaign.

"Every Christmas hundreds of accidents are caused by irresponsible women driving their so-called 'runabouts' down the wrong lane at 15mph, their brains addled by over-consumption," warned officer Bill Mason this morning.

"Other drivers must watch out for this menace," he added, "because we're far too busy running speed traps on the M1 to bother with it ourselves."

Greater Manchester POLICE

Arrest Warrant

Name Gina Adair
Age 59
Sex Indeterminate
Charge Conspiracy to commit crime within the jurisdiction of a police force not paying her associates to inform on each other to prevent such crime.

Pantomime cancelled

by our arts correspondent, John Blewitt

This year's Belfast pantomime, 'Stormont Dick and His Golden Nest-egg', has been cancelled due to a fire in the toilets.

"Oh no it hasn't," said a Northern Ireland Office spokesman yesterday. "Oh yes it has," said a DUP spokesman this morning.

The Portadown News

23RD DECEMBER 2003   www.PortadownNews.com

BRITISH NATIONAL PARTY
Exciting reader offer!

Win a year's subscription to 'White Trash' magazine by completing this simple tie-breaker:

British nationalism differs from Irish nationalism because

_____

_____

_____

Sandy Row Tanning Salon

Caution: dark tans may be hazardous

LETTERS TO THE EDITOR

A Chara

It is obvious that the bombing of Dublin and Monaghan in 1973 was the work of anti-Irish bigots within the security forces. Everybody knows that Protestants are too stupid to build car bombs.

Is Mise

Anne Phoblacht, West Belfast

Dear Sir

The accusation that I planted the Monaghan bomb is completely untrue. Everybody knows that I was driving some nuns to an Alliance Party meeting at the time.

Yours sincerely

Billy Shootspatrick, Portadown News

Notice to the Editor

To prevent the possibility of legal action arising from the publication of the Barron Report, any attempt by you to publish the Barron Report will result in immediate legal action. Please destroy this letter.

Ministry of Defence, Whitehall

Dear Sir

This matter belongs before a court, as I said when I parked my car bomb outside the Old Bailey.

Yours insincerely

Gerry Kelly, North Belfast

Simply a simple mistake

by our unionist correspondent, Will March

The Ulster Unionist Party has denied that its assembly election campaign raised racial tensions in The Village.

"We apologise for any confusion our 'British People Eat Fish and Chips' posters may have caused," said a UUP spokesman yesterday.

"In fact the people of Ulster and Hong Kong have a great deal in common, such as being governed by Chris Patten without electing him, and being handed over to a foreign country without our permission."

FAMINE THREATENS VILLAGE

by our loyalist correspondent, Billy Shootspatrick

FAMINE will strike Belfast's Village neighbourhood if more Chinese people are expelled from the area, health officials have warned.

Local resident Shelley-Anne McAvoy (17) confirmed that hunger is already affecting her household. "Our Tyler hasn't had his bitter and sour pork fat with gravy fried lard and extra chips for three days," she said. "He's wasting away before my very eyes."

The Sandy Row UVF remains unrepentant. "Chinese people are known for their hard work, family values and excellent exam results," said a spokesman yesterday. "This is a clear provocation to loyalists everywhere."

Black Santa warning

by our retail correspondent, Kaye Mart

Loyalists have warned Belfast's 'Black Santa' to stay out of The Village. "It's bad enough that he's Church of Ireland," said a UDA spokesman yesterday, "but to be black as well is the final insult." However local children have expressed confusion at the move. "My dad says our presents come from the white Santa," explained 5-year-old Tyler McAvoy, "but my mum says they come from the black market."

SILENCE FROM MARS STORY

by our science correspondent, Bunsen Burns

Ulsterman Jack Russell, mission controller on the ill-fated Bassett 2 Mars probe, has lost contact with the Belfast Telegraph.

"All last week we had regular contact with the Telegraph," confirmed Mr Russell yesterday. "We received headlines such as 'Jack is out of this world', 'Jack is star of the show' and 'Tenuous local connection to national news story', but since then we've heard nothing."

Radio telescopes are now searching for a mention on Talkback.

Laird o' the Rings

The expensive fantasy with its own made-up language

Christmas

PORTADOWN NEWS ANNUAL CHRISTMAS APPEAL

At this special time of year, our thoughts naturally turn to those less fortunate than ourselves. In the spirit of the season, the Portadown News asks its readers to support the 'Imagine Belfast' Christmas Appeal.

Hundreds of people are now facing an uncertain future after the disastrous famine of ideas which struck Imagine Belfast throughout its entire existence. Many thought they had secure employment until well after 2008, and bought ridiculously expensive riverfront apartments which are now worthless due to a recent outbreak of culture in the Short Strand. Please give generously, because if these people aren't supported then they'll just come up with another lunatic scam that will end up costing us all a fortune.

DRINK & DRIVE WARNING

by our crime correspondent, Rob Berry

Speaking at the launch of this year's 'Don't Drink and Drive' campaign, PSNI Officer Bill Mason urged Christmas party-goers to leave their cars at home.

'If you're celebrating with a drink, don't drive,' said Officer Mason. 'Rely instead on a taxi driver who's been working continuously for 96 hours by injecting speed directly into his heart.'

The students are back!

by our student correspondent, Grant Dole

Portadown's pubs and bars are bracing themselves for a busy few weeks, as hundreds of students return home to spend Christmas with their laundry.

'It's always great when the students are back,' local barman Tony McConville told our reporter yesterday. 'I just can't wait to hear another 400 stories about clubbing in Dundee.'

New Year

New Year Resolution suggestions

David Trimble
I promise to be more polite

Danny Morrison
I promise to take a writing course

Catriona Ruane
I promise to shave every day

Peter Robinson
I promise not to laugh at the funeral

It's been another great year for our great little town!

by our sarcasm correspondent, Jesus O'Reilly

Some say a year is an arbitrary period of time with no special significance, but here at The Portadown News we think otherwise!

That's because we've been told to put together a Review of the Year Special Issue, forcing us to retrospectively impose a narrative structure on what was basically just some stuff that happened.

But hey – that's journalism for you.

Great year for tourism

by our tourism correspondent, W. G. Bribe

Portadown's tourist industry went from strength to strength this year, with Tourism Board chiefs investing millions of pounds in themselves.

'We're putting the unfortunate scandals of earlier in the year behind us,' said a Tourist Board spokesman at yesterday's launch of the board's latest brochure, entitled 'Portadown: A Great Place to Print a Brochure'.

NEW YEAR BABIES BORN

by whichever reporter was unlucky enough to be on duty when this old chestnut rolled around again

SAOIRSE O'CHUCKY
"She was delivered, as one day Ireland will be delivered," says proud mum Catriona.

BILLY CARSON
"I was booked in for a caesarean, but he took the traditional route," says proud mum Kelly-Anne.

TYLER HOOD
"Watch he doesn't lift your camera, mister," says proud mum Kylie.

BEN CARRYDUFF
"Ben is a very lucky boy," says proud mum Mary. "His dad's name is on his birth certificate."

As Gaeilge or else

Today's compulsory Irish lesson, with moderate SDLP Councillor Patsy McGlone

In the planter tongue	As Gaeilge
We fully respect your culture	Tiocfaidh Ar La
Parity of esteem is very important	Tiocfaidh Ar La
Protestants are valued and respected	Tiocfaidh Ar La
Triumphalist sectarianism? No thanks!	Tiocfaidh Ar La
Please stop voting for Sinn Fein	Tiocfaidh Ar La

FARMERS UP IN ARMS

South Armagh residents group 'Farmers Who Are Obviously Provos' has demanded an end to Imperial Stormtrooper patrols in the area.

"They're frightening the mynocks, putting the tauntauns off their feed and making the bantha milk taste funny," said a spokesman yesterday. "If they don't go back to their own planet I'll put my tractor beam on them."

THE PORTADOWN NEWS

GALAXY LONG AGO, FAR AWAY EDITION. NOT FOR SALE IN LURGAN.

Donaldson joins the Dark Side

by our robot correspondent, Anne Droid

A terrible disturbance was felt across Northern Ireland yesterday, as if a million voices suddenly cried out in terror and were suddenly silenced, as Jedi Donaldson finally crossed over to the Dark Side.

"Patience, young Sky-Faulkner"

"Give in to your hate! Feel your power grow stronger!" said Mr Donaldson in an interview with the Lisburn Death Star.

Doc Vader, Lord of the Dark Side, introduced his latest recruit at a press conference this morning. "The rebels will never defeat us now," he said. "May the Third Force be with you!"

Unavailable for comment, Yoda was.

Spacer invader

by our security correspondent, Roger Base

Dark Side deputy Peter Robinson has denied reports that he was involved in an Attack of the Clones.

"It wasn't Clones," said Mr Robinson yesterday, "it was Clontibret."

ON OTHER PAGES
Ewok-Wookie incident 'not sectarian' ...p57
New pictures of Sammy Wilson's moon ...p57

A personal message from Doc Vader to the people of Northern Ireland

I am your father now

AT-AT Walkers demand right to march

The Portadown News

20TH JANUARY 2004 | www.PortadownNews.com

What now for the agreement?

We ask some leading politicians for their position on the review

PETER ROBINSON

"The agreement must be changed. The government can't change the agreement to save it."

GERRY ADAMS

"The agreement can't be changed. The government must change the agreement to save it."

Another legitimate protest

by our loyalist correspondent, Billy Shootspatrick

RIOTING loyalists at Maghaberry Prison have destroyed fridges, cookers, microwaves, snooker tables, gym equipment, a jacuzzi, a cinema, both swimming pools and a rare Japanese bonsai tree in the David Ervine memorial meditation garden.

Staff contained the disturbance using strong language under the supervision of Amnesty International, however inmates also set fire to the cappuccino bar before returning to their cells to plot another pipe bomb attack on a prison officer's wife.

The Northern Ireland Office has described the situation as "Back to normal".

¡PEPITAS DA GALINHA!

The exciting new column for the town's Portuguese community

Você sabe quando você diz que, "I am from Lisbon," e os locals dizem, "You're from Lisburn?" e você dizo, "No. L-I-S-B-O-N." Stupido.

Assim – £2.50 por a hora em May Pork, eh? Bastardos!

NORTEL DECLARES CEASE-HIRE

by our business correspondent, Reg Empty

RATHCOOLE electronics company Nortel has declared a cease-hire, however the organisation insists that it will not disband.

"We must all move forward," said a spokesman yesterday. "There is plenty of work still to be done – but not by us."

Sinn Fein described the statement as 'a complete breach of copyright'.

Paisley says 'No' to Europe

by our European correspondent, Ann Twerp

Ian Paisley has announced his retirement from European politics.

"I shall be returning to Northern Ireland to lead the fight against Peter Robinson," said Mr Paisley. "He needn't think he's getting away with anything!" The decision marks the end of a distinguished 25-year career in Brussels.

That distinguished career in full:

1979 – Elected to the European Parliament

1988 – Called the Pope a bastard

2004 – Quit the European Parliament

"Let's face it, that's more than I've done," admitted fellow MEP John Hume yesterday.

PORTADOWN NEWS INFOBOX

This week: Why a former RUC officer might join Sinn Fein

1. Higher salary, faster car, cheaper drugs
2. Even better chance of owning a pub
3. No more hassle from Nuala O'Loan
4. Closer contact with Special Branch
5. SDLP being phased out under Patten

ANTI-SOCIAL BEHAVIOUR

THEFT

VANDALISM

ASSAULT

OFFENSIVE LANGUAGE

The reality is...

LOITERING

Portadown News Letter

PUTTING THE PROD BACK INTO PROTESTANT

Are you ashamed to be protestant? Then this is the paper for you, because the Portadown News Letter is committed to restoring the confidence that protestants enjoyed before they read this editorial. We will celebrate the tolerance, freedom and diversity of our community by defining its values in a short list scribbled on the back of a napkin. Values like:

Religion
You're not a protestant without one.

Heritage
It's not just for fenians.

Politics
Especially office politics.

The campaign to rebuild protestant confidence starts today. The campaign to sack the editor starts tomorrow. God Save the Queen!

Paisley breaks the ice

If my daughter wrote a book like that I'd throw her out of the house

---

Inland Revenue

SELF-ASSESSMENT TAX FORM - PLEASE COMPLETE BY EASTER 2016

NAME: _Gerry Adams_   TRADING AS: _Sinn Fein - IRA_

SELF-EMPLOYED ☐   SELF-DEPLOYED ☐   ON CESSATION ☒

DO YOU OWN YOUR OWN SAFE-HOUSE?   YES ☒   NO ☐

OFF-SHORE ASSETS	INCOME: £ _300 a week, plus benefits_
NORAID	EXPENSES
Rita O'Hare	TAXIS: £ ← _Isn't this income as well?_
OFF-SHORE LIABILITIES	DIESEL: £
Colombia Three	DECLARATION
Rita O'Hare	_Tiocfaidh ar la!_

Meaningless threat shock

by our loyalist correspondent, Billy Shootspatrick

Government funding for loyalist groups will be cut if racist violence continues, warned the Loyalist Funding Commission yesterday. "Grants will be withheld immediately," said a Commission spokesman. "This money is only to be used for attacking Catholics."

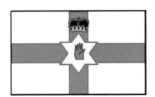

PORTADOWN NEWS INFOBOX

Why loyalists are using marine flares as pipe bombs:

1. Had them lying around the yacht anyway
2. Easy to buy in Larne, Bangor and Carrickfergus
3. All the nice boys love a sailor
4. Bright orange colour goes with sash
5. Also useful when you're hopelessly adrift

FOOT & MOUTH – FARMER'S INCOMES HIT

by our agriculture correspondent, Culchie McMucker

The foot & mouth crisis deepened yesterday, when Tandragee farmer Josias Bogman was forced to buy a new 2.8-litre Range Rover instead of the 3.5 TDi model he really wanted.

"I feel stunned and demoralised," Mr Bogman told our reporter, "and the most heartbreaking thing of all is watching the effect this has had on my wife. She just knows that the girls at the golf club will be laughing at her, and it's threatening to tear our family apart."

Although the 2.8-litre petrol and 3.5-litre turbo diesel Range Rovers offer similar performance, farmers prefer the larger model.

"The 3.5 delivers higher pollution and better tax avoidance, and it's also slightly more annoying to be stuck behind at 40mph," explained Mr Bogman. "Now, get off my land."

PORTADOWN NEWS INFOBOX

Why the RVH car park fiasco is "Good for patients"

1. Low-income families have the worst health
2. This is because poor people are fat and lazy
3. Walking is the best exercise
4. So walking to hospital targets the needy
5. Sure, they just spend their money on fags anyway.

Question 1

The results of a public consultation exercise on abolishing the 11-plus are:

35% for abolition
65% against abolition

How many years should you wait before ignoring these results?

A: 1 year
B: 2 years
C: 5 years

DUP proposals unveiled

by our unionist correspondent, Will March

The DUP has unveiled its devolution proposals, and admit it, you've already stopped reading. You know rightly they'll all sit down and cobble something together but frankly you're long past caring about the details. It's got something to do with having committees instead of ministers, isn't that right? I suppose it'll keep them off the streets.

Of course Sinn Fein will kick up a stink but then again don't they always. They'll step up to trough in the end though, just like the rest of them. Anyway what's on the other side?

Poetry Corner

www.PortadownNews.com

Submitted by 'Sarge', *The Hood National Anthem –* (*to be sung to the tune of "American Pie"*)

Long, long time ago, I can still remember how
  those hoodin' gubbers made me laugh
And I know if I had a chance to see those baps and
  jantys dance, I'd
laugh my arse off once again.
'Cos don't they realise it's not clever,
Drinking Bucky down the river, Tucked-in
  tracksuit bottoms, They look just f**kin' ratten!
I can't remember if I cried when saw these
  slabbers all whacked and fried
But it amused me deep inside . . .
The day the Bucky thrived!

And they were singin'. . .
Bye, bye, eatin' spuds cheapest pie,
Drove the Uno roun' the town oh wi' the techno
  up high,
Wearing baseball caps though it's nearly July
*Singin', "I'll stick this f**kin' knife in yer eye*
*. . . I'll stick this f**kin' knife in yer eye!"*

Did you write the book of shite?
"Here len'is ten bob, gonna gizza light?"
Did ya call my Da a Bast**d!?
Oh and do you believe in hard core techno?
Have ye gubbed 5 E's in the back of a Metro?
And can you teach me how to speak reeeaaallll fast?!
You can tell that she's in love wi' him,
Cos he's a Jaffa and she's a Tim,
They kicked off filthy socks and those manky old
  Reeboks.
He was a scrawny youth with a GAP pullover,
A sovrin ring and a stolen Nova,
They fell in love when he muff dived 'er, (sorry!)
The day the Bucky thrived. . .

And they were singin'. . .
Bye, bye, eatin' spuds cheapest pie,
Drove the Uno roun' the town oh wi' the techno
  up high,
Wearing baseball caps though it's nearly July
*Singin', "I'll stick this f**kin' knife in yer eye*
*. . . I'll stick this f**kin' knife in yer eye!"*

Now for ten years you've been on the dole,
Claimin' off the DOE, coz ya fell doun a hole
And that's just how it's always been.
When the headcase screamed at the Police van,
In a coat he'd stolen from TopMan,
And a fag that came from you or me
But while the peeler was looking dapper,
The wheel brace hit him on the napper,
Dressed all in Kappa clobber,
As he shouted, "suck ma wabber!"
While wee Sean stole shoes from Clarks',
And Billy slashed some bum in the park,
They all sniffed petrol in the dark,
The day the Bucky thrived . . .

And they were singin'. . .
Bye, bye, eatin' spuds cheapest pie,
Drove the Uno roun' the town oh wi' the techno
  up high,
Wearing baseball caps though it's nearly July
*Singin', "I'll stick this f**kin' knife in yer eye*
*. . . I'll stick this f**kin' knife in yer eye!"*

Yer NO FEAR sticker is a belter
Writing mentions on the old bus shelter,
Eight days straight drinking Faaaaaaaaaast!

Doin' six months fer selling black,
The chip pan diet and the heart attack
A night out at Space wi' the hack.
The millies reek of cheap perfume,
While name-tag necklaces jangle round the room,
Face like a well bashed cheezer
A fag and lemon Breezer.
The lack of class is hard to hide,
They just can't wait to get inside,
An ink tattoo and a door-way ride,
That's how the punters thrive.

And they were singin' . . .
Bye, bye, eatin' spuds cheapest pie,
Drove the Uno roun' the town oh wi' the techno
* up high,*
Wearing baseball caps though it's nearly July
*Singin', "I'll stick this f**kin' knife in yer eye*
*. . . I'll stick this f**kin' knife in yer eye!"*

You'll see them in their usual places,
With baseball hats and ugly faces,
Outside the offy acting hard.
So Shug be nimble, Shug be quick,
And get an ounce of speed on tick
Then cut it up and sell it to yer mates.
All lined up outside the "Paki's",
A rainbow of exotic trackies,
Givin' abuse to all grannies,
Ya f**ked up bunch of fannies!
And as the day turns into night,
The hoods may gang up to start a fight,
But on their own they're soft as shite!
That day the Old Firm tied.

And they were singin' . . .
Bye, bye, eatin' spuds cheapest pie,
Drove the Uno roun' the town oh wi' the techno
* up high,*
Wearing baseball caps though it's nearly July
*Singin', "I'll stick this f**kin' knife in yer eye*
*. . . I'll stick this f**kin' knife in yer eye!"*

(Slowly with feeling)
I met a girl who sang 'The Sash',
I asked about her f**kin' moustache,
But she just told me to f**k off!
I went down to the local chippy,
Where the hoods hung out and the staff were nippy,
And the punters there
Harassed me for some fags.
Baseball hats at stupid angles,
The girls each wore three dozen bangles,
Hair done up with scrunchies,
Munching crisps and Crunchies.
But the three meals they enjoy the most,
Are chinkies, chippies, beans on toast,
Come Belfast fair they hit the coast,
Those days the Bucky thrives!

And they were singin' . . .
Bye, bye, eatin' spuds cheapest pie,
Drove the Uno roun' the town oh wi' the techno
* up high,*
Wearing baseball caps though it's nearly July
*Singin', "I'll stick this f**kin' knife in yer eye*
*. . . I'll stick this f**kin' knife in yer eye!"*

Some lines in remembrance of the Real IRA volunteers who have fallen this week in the fields of France

If others should have to die, it will not occur to me
That there's some corner of an Irish field
That is for ever Ireland. There shall be
In that rich earth a richer dust concealed;
A dust whom Ireland bore, shaped, made aware,
Gave once her flowers to love, her ways to Rome,
A body of Ireland's, breathing Irish air,
Blown to smithereens by our own brave sons of home.

Poetry Corner

Garvaghy group publishes poetry

by our women's features reporter, Gail Tinkerbell

The Garvaghy Road Organisation for Women's Literature (GROWL) has published a new book of poetry by Portadown women.

"The Rape of Ireland: 1,000 Years of Violation" brings together the work of over 15 housewives from the Ballyoran area, to express in verse their thoughts and images of Irish history.

"Only women can fully understand Ireland in the context of historical physicality," GROWL Chairperson Dervla Drabble told me over Carlsberg and Hobnobs in her Churchill Park residence yesterday. "Ireland is the woman, while Britain is her male oppressor. The Mull of Kintyre, for example, is an obscene phallus held menacingly over the Fair Head, ready to be thrust into the moist harbour of Belfast Lough."

The book has already received rave reviews in An Phoblacht, The Andersonstown News and The Guardian. But Ms Drabble is most proud of the introduction supplied personally by Sinn Fein leader and poetry buff Gerry Adams.

"Women have always been central to the struggle for Irish freedom," writes Mr Adams. "When you've been out smuggling diesel all day, it's important to know that your dinner's on the table."

Some lines on the disbandment of the IRA
by Danny 'Yeats' Morrison

I have met them at close of day
Coming with masked faces
From pub and bar among grey
Housing Executive houses.

I have given the nod and the wink
Or polite menacing words
Or have lingered a while and said
'We know where you live'.

Too long a sacrifice
Can make a Stormont of the heart
O when may it suffice?
That is Gerry's part, our part

All changed utterly, utterly butterly
A terrorist beauty contest is born.

Lines on the demolition of Seamus Heaney's house
'DIGGER'

Between the developer and his gain
My old house sits; open to the rain
Through the broken window, an engine's sound
The JCB moves forward along the ground
My house, collapsing. I look down
As walls rain in lumps from the bedrooms
And fall below, approximately twenty yards
away
To the rhythm of the pneumatic drills
Where I was living
By God. Yer man can sure handle a digger.
Just like his old man.

Travel News

Peter Robinson to be privatised?

by our transport correspondent, Fred Petrolhead

TRANSLINK has announced that Transport Minister Peter Robinson may be privatised. 'We believe that Mr Robinson would provide a much better service if he was removed from the public sector,' said a Translink spokesman yesterday.

However Mr Robinson's party has hit back. 'The Minister has successfully integrated pro- and anti-Agreement routes from a single platform,' said a DUP spokesman this morning, 'allowing our supporters to travel in both directions simultaneously.'

NEW RAIL LINK PLANNED

by our transport correspondent, Fred Petrolhead

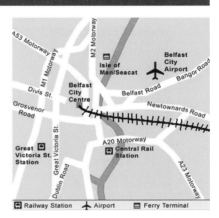

Transport Minister Peter Robinson has announced that Belfast's first-ever light rail link will run from the city centre along the Newtownards Road to Castlereagh.

"This exciting new project will benefit both sections of the community," he told our reporter yesterday, "by which I mean the people who vote for me, and the people who vote for my wife."

Major investment for town!

by our business correspondent, Reg Empty

PORTADOWN'S crumbling infrastructure received a much-needed boost this week with the opening of a new bus-shelter at Market Street. The £400 million project will be paid for by charging people to flush their own toilets.

'It's often claimed that public transport is money down the drain,' said Mayor Alice Maskey yesterday, 'and where better than Portadown to put that philosophy into practice? The new bus-shelter also provides a fully-integrated transport facility for the town, as both Protestants and Catholics will be allowed to use it.' (Except Sundays)

The Portadown News

10TH FEBRUARY 2004   www.PortadownNews.com

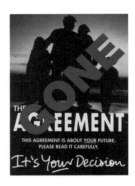

PRAGUE FLIGHT BOOST

by our European correspondent, Ann Twerp

The new direct flight from Belfast to Prague will boost Northern Ireland's economy, say business leaders.
"You can already bring drugs straight back from Amsterdam," said one local entrepreneur yesterday, "and now you'll be able to bring Semtex straight back from the Czech Republic."

Government outlaws hatred

by our crime correspondent, Rob Berry

OPPRESSED GROUPS across Northern Ireland were celebrating last night after the government's historic decision to abolish hatred.

New hate-crime legislation will ban the terms 'Fenian', 'Poof' and 'Fenian Poof' although 'Black Bastard' may still be used when addressing police officers.

"This new hate-crime law is certain to be just as successful as every other law against crime in Northern Ireland," said one jubilant member of the Belfast Anti-Racist-Sexist-Sectarian-Homophobic Network.

"In the unlikely event of anyone being prosecuted for a hate-crime, they can expect to serve just under half of their slightly increased sentence," warned a PSNI spokesman yesterday.

BLOODY DE LOREAN INQUIRY

Lord Saville:	So who was fired first?
Employee F:	Totally innocent workers.
Lord Saville:	Who was ultimately responsible?
Lawyer 361:	The British government!
Lord Saville:	Fair enough. Let's adjourn for £150 million.
Next week:	The New Lodge £6 Billion Inquiry

New Euro-candidates announced

Morris Minor, DUP	**Dirk Markedman, SDLP**	**Barbie Brownshirt, Sinn Fein**
		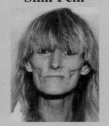
Believes Europe is a papal plot. Wants more money for farmers.	Believes a united Europe means a united Ireland. Wants more money for farmers.	Believes Germany has a solution to our problems. Wants to borrow some cattle-trucks.

PORTADOWN NEWS INFOBOX

Why the NIO locks asylum seekers up in Maghaberry

1. Protects them from hate-crime

2. In line with segregation policy

3. Handy for Aldergrove

4. Crumlin Road jail still on fire

Ulster prattler

John Hume's retirement party

On other pages...

Rival factions meet at Stormont

Dodds outlines party principles

Horse's arse entertains crowd

Jobs blow for North West

by our business correspondent, Reg Empty

Londonderry's only employer, Bloody Sunday Inquiries Ltd, is to close with the loss of 6,000 jobs. The company is blaming global market conditions for the shock decision.

"Life is simply much cheaper abroad," explained a management spokesman yesterday. "When a Rwandan gets killed it only costs half a Red Cross parcel and a visit from Princess Anne. We just can't compete with those sort of prices."

Staff were in tears today as they left the factory gates by chauffeur-driven limousine. "It's devastating news, especially this close to Christmas," said one employee adding, "My fee for that quote is £800."

Should there be a Truth Commission?

Morris Minor, DUP	Barbie Brownshirt, Sinn Fein	Fin Madden, Solicitor
	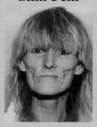	
Yes – but only if it focuses exclusively on terrorism	Yes – but only if it focuses exclusively on collusion	YES! YES! YES!

BBC NEWSLINE

Have you got an opinion on today's news?
Then phone, text or e-mail us your half-baked notions
and we'll try reading them out with a straight face.

BERTIE AHERN VISITS OMAGH

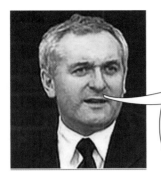

"It's a privilege to spend a few quiet moments here in the Omagh Remembrance Garden, before the victims' relatives arrive and start asking awkward questions. You know, every time I come to Omagh I ask myself a question: Couldn't they have put up some houses here instead? Maybe even an apartment building? I'm sure I could get the planning permission sorted out for a small consideration ... Christ, here come the relatives! Taxi! Taxi!"

BBC Northern Ireland — Hearts & Minds

Noel Thompson	Good evening, Mr Adams
Gerry Adams	I have not come here to discuss the goodness of the evening.
Noel Thompson	I'm sorry ...
Gerry Adams	Look, the reality is that the time has come for others to move beyond the politics of apologising.
Noel Thompson	Well then, if I could just ...
Gerry Adams	Just? Just? What's 'just' about this anti-Sinn Fein agenda inherent in this line of questioning?

... and so on

UNIVERSITY STRIKE CRISIS

by our education correspondent, Una O'Level

A recent survey of journalists reveals that the university strike is causing a serious shortage of recent surveys.

"How are we going to fill these feature pages?" asked one editor yesterday. "We haven't seen a press release about obesity, social exclusion or falling sperm counts all week."

Annan comments on securocrat crisis

Don't worry - nobody's listening to you

HOLY F**K IT'S SNOWING

by our weather correspondent, Michael Foul

NORTHERN IRELAND was plunged into chaos this week as just under two inches of powdery snow settled gently on elevated ground. Roads were blocked five months earlier than usual and hundreds of schools closed amid fears that children's brains might freeze.

"I would advise people to panic," the Secretary of State told reporters yesterday. "Northern Ireland has become a cold house for everybody."

EMERGENCY PATCH OF SNOW HOTLINE
Have you seen a patch of snow in your area?
Call 028-90-DAYOFF immediately.

PSNI in 'unacceptable tattoo' shock

Who will replace David Trimble?

Reg Humpy (2-1 favourite)

"I'm not Jeffrey Donaldson – and that still counts for something."

Lord Looney (65-1 odd)

"I can only support myself to an extent that suggests serious reservations."

David Sideburn (own clear favourite)

"David Trimble is hugely unpopular – and that's my job."

Political crisis latest:

Scumbags beat up scumbag – no normal people hurt

see page 42

Water cannon worry

by our security correspondent, Roger Base

The police will fit special equipment to their new water cannons to prevent them firing hard water, it has been announced.

"This will make the water cannons compatible with our soft soap policy," explained PSNI officer Bill Mason yesterday. "It will also help rioters to work up a lather."

The new water cannons will shortly be deployed on the Limescale Road.

PORTADOWN'S FAVOURITE COLUMNISTS!

Steven Queen

How can Bertie Ahern tell unionists to work with Gerry Adams? We all know that Fianna Fail isn't too fond of sharing power itself. The Taoiseach must understand that unionists expect him to make no distinction between north and south …

… and so on

Judith Collins

How dare Bertie Ahern call Gerry Adams a liar! We all know that Fianna Fail isn't too fond of telling the truth itself. The Taoiseach must understand that nationalists expect him to stay down south, keep his mouth shut and let us run the north our own way …

… and so on

TELEVISION CLASSICS
This week: The Irish Chief Constable

EPISODE 1 'THE BIG HOUSE'

"Would you like me to bring the water cannon around now sir?" asked Slipper. "Yes please," said the Irish Chief Constable, "and ask Mrs Cadogan to clean the conservatory, the sun lounge, the en-suite jacuzzi, the swimming pool, the outdoor hot tub, the double garage with upstairs games room, the helipad, the fifth guest bedroom, the built-in sauna …

… continued up to a value of £700,000 (or nearest offer)

THE IRISH C.C.

E.Œ.Somerville & Martin Ross

The Portadown News

9TH MARCH 2004

www.PortadownNews.com

Home Office
New drug classifications

Class A
Ecstasy

Class B
Speed

Class C
Cannabis

Class 5C,
Portadown High
All of the above

George Mitchell in Disney job shock

Where's Goofy?

Lisburn

ADAMS MOURNS FELLOW-TRAVELLERS
by our denial correspondent, D. Niall

A MAN who denies being in the IRA has denied any links to the organisation which denies bombing Madrid. Mr Gerald Adams (67), who denies being 67, denied requests for an interview yesterday but issued the following denial:

"I condemn those responsible for the appalling events of the past week, when some misguided individuals invited ETA's political wing to the Sinn Fein ard fheis. My thoughts and prayers are with the hundreds of photographs taken during this public relations atrocity. May they rest in peace."

Review of the review

David Trimble UUP	Ian Paisley DUP	Gerry Adams Sinn Fein

Will talk to Sinn Fein Won't stay in talks	Will stay in talks Won't talk to Sinn Fein	Will talk to anybody Won't tell the truth

RACIST LEAFLET SHAME

EXCLUSIVE: by our loyalist correspondent, Billy Shootspatrick

THE LOYALIST PEOPLE OF SOUTH BELFAST WILL NAT STAND FOR ANY MORE CHINESE IN OUR ~~NAYBORHOOD~~ ~~NAEBORHOOD~~ AREA, SO WE WON'T. THEY ARE THREATENING OUR WAY OF LIFE BY WORKING AND UNDERMINING OUR BRITISHNESS BY MAKING THE PLACE LOOK LIKE LONDON. THEY SHOULD ALL GO BACK TO JAPAN WHERE THEY CAME FROM, SO THEY SHOULD.
GOD SAVE THE QUEEN!

writing on the wall

Northlife sacks drummer

by our boyband correspondent, Darren Bumfluff

UNIONIST fans were distraught last night after David McTrimble announced that he was quitting Northlife.

"It's time for me to pursue a solo career," David told a crowd of fat 14-year-old girls yesterday. Former band-mates wished him well.

"Let's face it," said a record company spokesman, "David's been a lone voice for quite some time now."

Sinn Fein salutes Dublin government

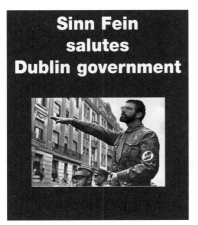

Meanwhile, in West Belfast

The Portadown News

23RD MARCH 2004

www.PortadownNews.com

Phoenix gas in 20% price rise shock

> You should have gone for oil mate

Sunday nags nag

by our religion correspondent, Helen Brimstone

Ian Paisley has warned Ulster Unionists not to bet on stalking horses on the Sabbath day.

"On Good Friday Jesus entered Jerusalem on a donkey while people threw palms," said the DUP leader yesterday. "Now the Ulster Unionists have entered a horse against David Trimble to palm off the Good Friday Agreement, but people won't be thrown!"

Dr Paisley is 78.

NEW TOOME BYPASS

NEW DUNDALK BYPASS

The Lynx Effect

It will let you down

Entire country mugged while bystanders watch

by our crime correspondent, Rob Berry

A small country was stabbed in the back this week while onlookers failed to intervene. Northern Ireland, 82, was out shopping when a knife-wielding thug approached and demanded the keys to its future.

"There were plenty of people watching but none of them would help me to tackle the criminal," said Northern Ireland yesterday. "Nobody even bothered calling the police, although I suppose that doesn't surprise me."

The stolen future was later found burnt out in Poleglass.

Trimble clings on

by our unionist correspondent, Will March

DAVID TRIMBLE has survived yet another leadership vote, wrote our reporter yesterday before submitting this article a full day before the count took place. "Thank God the Ulster Unionist Party is so predictable," said our reporter to himself, "or this Friday deadline would be a right nuisance."

Editorial sources are confident that the actual outcome is irrelevant anyway.

UUP pantomime stalking horse

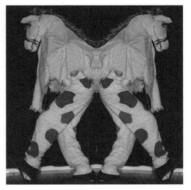

Where should we send the weapons inspectors?

Monaghan

Portadown News reader competition

Win two tickets to 'The Passion of the Christ'

Simply complete the following tie-breaker

Northern Ireland's church leaders have spent a hundred years picketing cinemas, calling for movies to be banned and blaming screen violence for all society's ills. But it's OK for their own congregations to watch a gory movie because

....

PORTADOWN NEWS INFOBOX

This week: Northern Ireland justice in action

■ Caught driving at 31mph in town – pay fine ■ Caught driving a bomb into Ballycastle – go free

Lookalikes

Sinn Fein's Conor Murphy in 'O'Brien' from Star Trek shock

Celine Dion in Iris Robinson shock

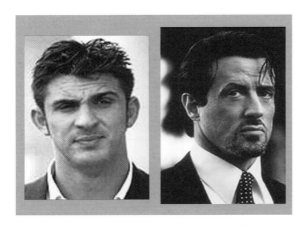

Andy Shoukri in Rambo shock

Gary McMichael in 'Men Behaving Badly' shock